PHILIP'S *Red Books* *showing th*

LOCAL STREET ATLAS

GLOUCESTER
CHELTENHAM
CIRENCESTER · STROUD

**BISHOPS CLEEVE · BROCKWORTH · CAM · NAILSWORTH
TETBURY · WINCHCOMBE · WOTTON-UNDER-EDGE**

CONTENTS

www.philips-maps.co.uk

First published in 2006 by
Estate Publications

This edition published by Philip's,
a division of Octopus Publishing Group Ltd
www.octopusbooks.co.uk
2–4 Heron Quays, London E14 4JP
An Hachette Livre UK Company

Second impression 2008
09/11-06

ISBN 978-0-540-09363-2

© Philip's 2008

This product includes mapping data licensed
from Ordnance Survey®, with the permission
of the Controller of Her Majesty's Stationery
Office.© Crown copyright 2006. All rights
reserved. Licence number 100011710

Minor Road

═══ Pedestrianized / Restricted Access

═══ Track

⌐ ⌐ Built Up Area

- - - - Footpath

∿∿ Stream

∿∿ River

Lock Canal

━■━ Railway / Station

● Post Office

P P+ Car Park / Park & Ride

C Public Convenience

✚ Place of Worship

→ One-way Street

i Tourist Information Centre

▲8 ▲8 Adjoining Pages

Area Depicting Enlarged Centre

Emergency Services

Industrial Buildings

Leisure Buildings

Education Buildings

Hotels etc.

Retail Buildings

General Buildings

Woodland

Orchard

Recreational / Parkland

Cemetery

CIRENCESTER
STROUD
Tetbury
Malmesbury
Cricklade
Purton
Wootton Bassett
Dursley
Nailsworth
Chipping Sodbury
Yate
Wotton-under-Edge
Stonehouse
Minchinhampton
Kemble
South Cerney
Siddington
Ashton Keynes
Minety
Sherston
Hullavington
Great Somerford
Brinkworth
Lydiard Millicent
Haydon Wick
Bisley
Chalford
Bussage
Brimscombe
Woodchester
Avening
Horsley
Uley
Cam
Coaley
Slimbridge
Frampton on Severn
Eastington
Leonard Stanley
Middleyard
Randwick
Pitchcombe
Upklands
Wickwar
Charfield
Badminton
Luckington
Didmarton
Kingscote
Beverston
Cherington
Rodmarton
Tarlton
Coates
Sapperton
Daglingworth
Baunton
Stratton
Poulton
Ampney Crucis
Ampney St. Mary
Ampney Park
Down Ampney
Latton
Marston Meysey
Driffield
Harnhill
Barnsley
Arlington
Ablington
North Cerney
Bagendon
Duntisbourne Rouse
Duntisbourne Abbots
Edgeworth
Sudgrove
Througham
Slad
Frampton Mansell
Oakley Wood
Hyde
Nympsfield
Ozleworth
North Nibley
Newport
Breadstone
Halmore
Purton
Awre
New Grounds
Tortworth
Cromhall
Cromhall Common
Engine Common
Horton
Little Sodbury
Old Sodbury
Dodington
Wapley
Hawkesbury
Hawkesbury Upton
Hillesley
Alderley
Tresham
Oldbury on the Hill
Leighterton
Westonbirt
Easton Grey
Shipton Moyne
Doughton
Tetbury Upton
Long Newnton
Brokenborough
Crudwell
Eastcourt
Hankerton
Charlton
Garsdon
Lea
Foxley
Corston
Norton
Alderton
Sopworth
Little Badminton
Acton Turville
Grittleton
Littleton Drew
Leigh Delamere
Stanton St. Quintin
Lower Stanton St. Quintin
Startley
Upper Seagry
Rodbourne
Dauntsey
Bradenstoke
Tockenham
Tockenham Wick
Grittenham
Callow Hill
Little Somerford
Cleverton
Upper Minety
Oaksey
Poole Keynes
Ewen
Culkerton
Ashley
Leigh
Green Hill
Hook
Purton Stoke
Cerney Wick
South Cerney Army Station
Frocester
Burton
Tormarton
R. Thames
Swill Brook
Derry Brook
Avon
MICHAEL WOOD
A429
A419
A433
A46
A4135
A38
A432
A3102
B4040
B4696
B4553
B4425
B4014
B4042
B4069
B4066
B4058
B4060
B4509
B4008
B4070
M4
M5

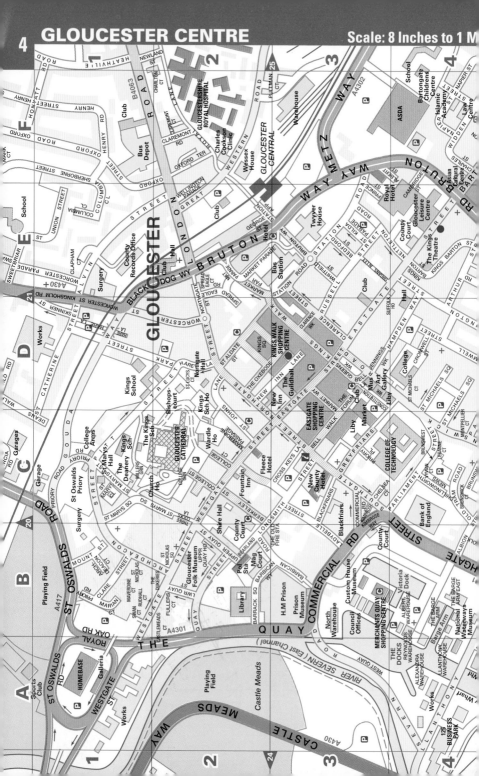

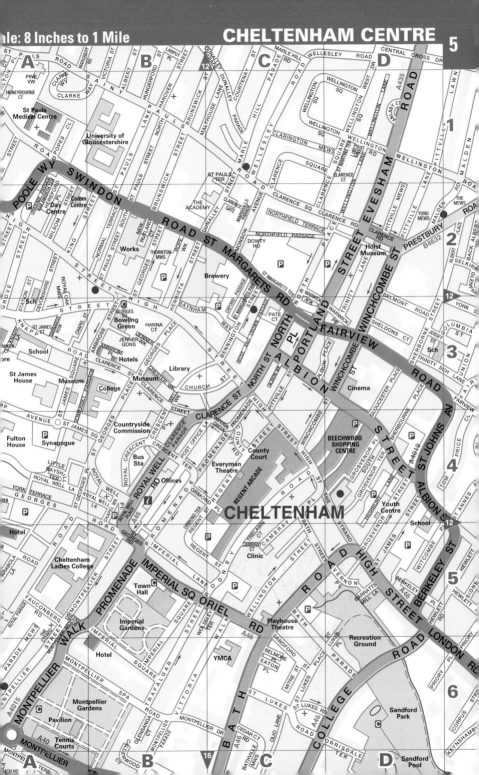

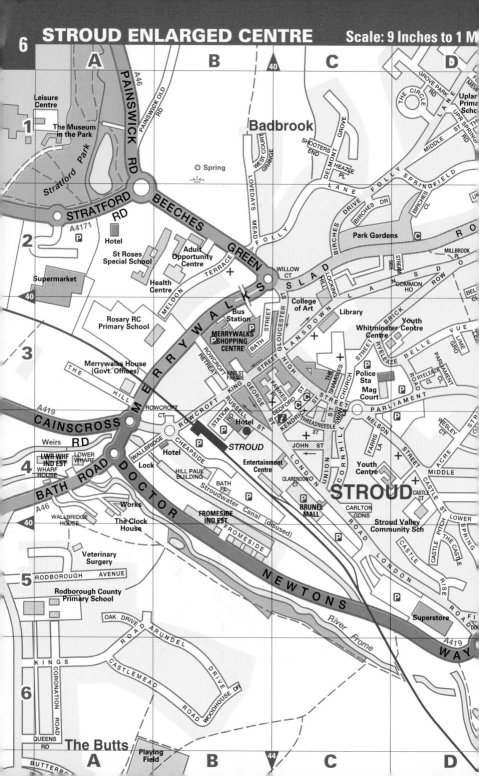

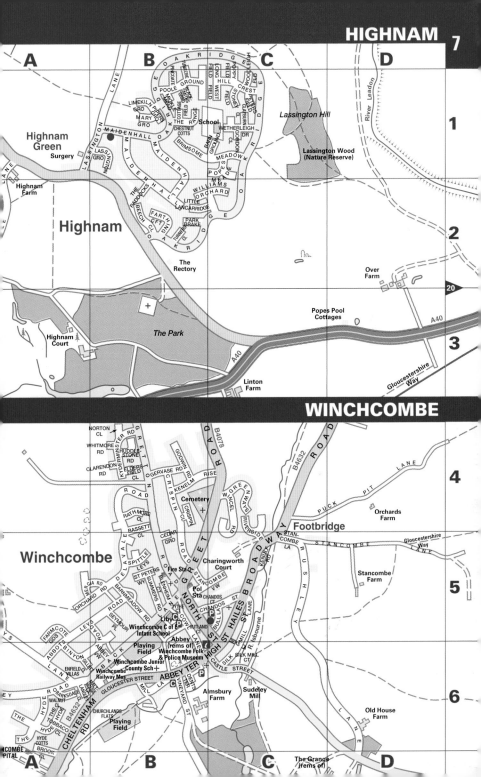

Highnam

Highnam Green

Highnam Farm

Surgery

Lassington Hill

Lassington Wood
(Nature Reserve)

River Leadon

School

Chestnut Cotts

The Rectory

Over Farm

Popes Pool Cottages

Highnam Court

The Park

Linton Farm

Gloucestershire Way

A40

20

Winchcombe

Cemetery

Footbridge

Orchards Farm

Gloucestershire Way

Charingworth Court

Fire Sta

Pol Sta

Stancombe Farm

Winchcombe C of E Infant School

Library

Abbey (rems of)

Winchcombe Folk & Police Museum

Playing Field

Winchcombe Junior County Sch

Winchcombe Railway Mus

Almsbury Farm

Sudeley Mill

Old House Farm

Playing Field

Churchlands Flats

The Grange (rems of)

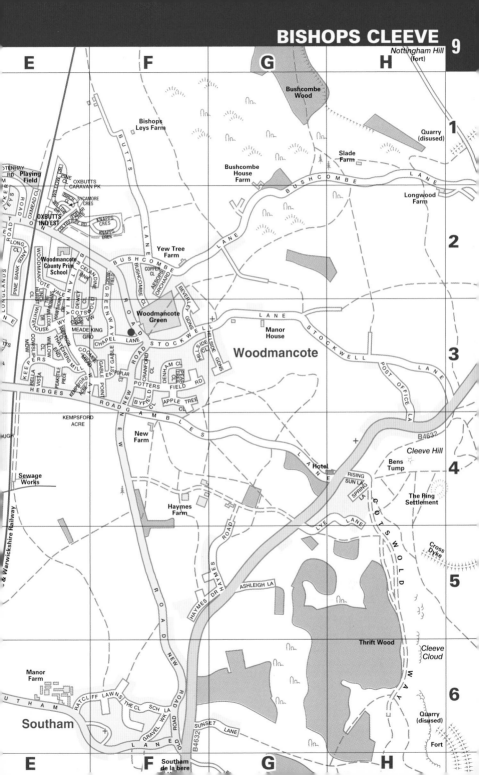

E   F   G   H

Nottingham Hill
(fort)

Bushcombe
Wood

Bishops
Leys Farm

Quarry
(disused)

1

Slade
Farm

Bushcombe
House
Farm

BUSHCOMBE   LANE

Longwood
Farm

Playing
Field

OXBUTTS
CARAVAN PK

PINE

SYCAMORE
CRES

OXBUTTS
IND EST

KNAPPS
CRES

KNAPPS
CRES

2

Woodmancote
County Prim
School

Yew Tree
Farm

COPPER

AISSOP

ORCHARD

BEVERLEY
GDNS

Woodmancote
Green

Manor
House

LANE

STOCKWELL

LANE

POST OFFICE LA

3

Woodmancote

MEADE KING
GRO

CHAPEL

LANE

STOCKWELL

ROAD

HILLSIDE
GDNS

KEMPSFORD
ACRE

New
Farm

GAMBLES

B4632

Cleve Hill

4

Sewage
Works

Haymes
Farm

Hotel

RISING
SUN LA

Bens
Tump

SPRING
LA

The Ring
Settlement

Cleve
Cloud

Cross
Dyke

5

HAYMES
DRIVE

ASHLEIGH LA

COTSWOLD

ROAD

NEW

ROAD

Thrift Wood

6

Manor
Farm

RATCLIFF LAWNS

THE CL

SCH LA

GRAVEL WK

Southam

SUNSET
LANE

Quarry
(disused)

Fort

Southam
de la bere

B4632

E   F   G   H

A B C D

TEWKESBURY

A4019

SHELDON COTTS
Sheldon Nurseries

M5 JUNCTION 10

Boddington Manor

1

WITHYBRIDGE GARDENS

WITHYBRIDGE LANE

Withy Bridge

CHURCH VW

Boddington

2

M5

Boddington House

Manor Farm

Mc

Old Hall

Butlers Court

Boddington Coppice

BUTLERS COTTS

Withy Bridge

Uckington

3

WITHYBRIDGE LANE

Millhouse Farm

River Chelt

Pilgrove Farm

4

WITHYBRIDGE

GLOUCESTER RO

Hayden Hill

1 HA
2 TH
3 SH

House in the Tree PH

Hope Farm

ROAD OLD

Orchard House

5

GLOUCESTER

ROAD

HAYDEN

Hayden Farm

Whitehall Farm

LANE

ATHERSTONE

Staverton Court

6

GLOUCESTER

ROAD OLD

Hayden

Hayden Green

HENLEY

HARTBURY
ETTINGTON
CL

SPRINGBANK

HENLEY RD

SPRINGBO

SPRINGBANK RD

LE C

B4634

STER

LANE HAYDEN

Water Pollution Control Centre

Fiddlers Green

SPRIN

A B 14 C D

E   **F**   **G**   **H**

Chosen View Farm

Church Farm

Fairoaks

1

Home Farm

Chestnut Farm

Playing Fields

Uckington Farm

2

Ho m

Swindon

Swindon Manor

Swindon Hall

Manor Farm

Engine Works

Playing Fields

Nurseries

INDUSTRIAL ESTATE

3

Nurseries

Swindon Farm

GALLAGHER RETAIL PARK

MANOR PARK BUSINESS CENTRE

SHAFTSBURY INDUSTRIAL ESTATE

Sports Ground

Club

Supermarket

Wks

GLOUCESTER

GALLAGHER RETAIL PK

Kingsditch

4

Jursery

River Chelt

School

Schools

KINGSDITCH RETAIL PK

INDUSTRIAL ESTATE

Wks

SHOPPING CENTRE

Springfield Ho

Pavilion

KINGSDITCH RETAIL PK

INDUSTRIAL ESTATE

12

Playing Field

Old Peoples Home

KINGSMEAD

Works

KINGSMEAD IND EST

MANCHESTER PARK

St P

5

Schs

PROVIDENCE PARK

Arle
BROOKLYN CT

Tewkesbury Bridge

Wks

ngbank

School

Hesters Way

School

CHELTENHAM INDUSTRIAL PARK

6 Work

Schools

Arle Road Bridge

Als He College

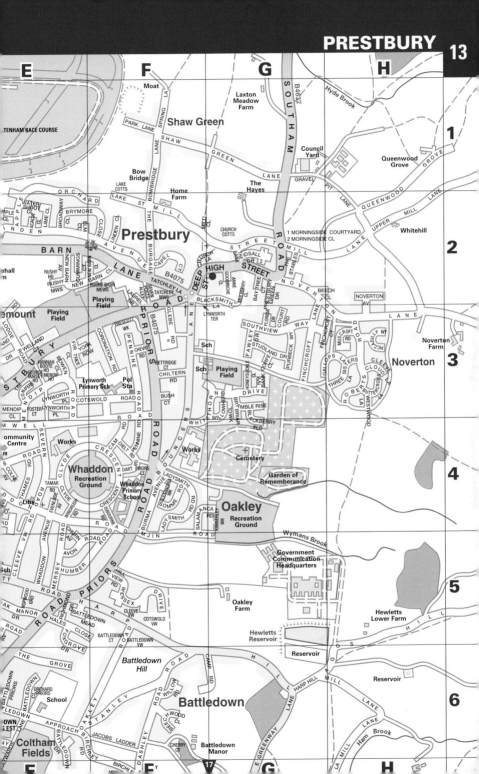

E   F   G   H

1

CHELTENHAM RACE COURSE

Moat

Laxton
Meadow
Farm

Hyde Brook

B4632

SOUTHAM

Shaw Green

PARK LANE

SPRING LANE

SHAW

GREEN

LANE

Council
Yard

GRAVEL

PIT

Queenwood
Grove

GROVE

QUEENWOOD

UPPER MILL LANE

Bow
Bridge

LAKE
COTTS

BOWBRIDGE

Home
Farm

The
Hayes

ROAD

Whitehill

ORCHARD

LAKE ST

THE MILL

CHURCH
COTTS

STREET

1 MORNINGSIDE COURTYARD
2 MORNINGSIDE CL

WATER
SHOOT
CL

BRYMORE

BROADWAY

LIME CL

ELM

CLOSE AVENUE

BURGAGE

CAPEL

CHURCH
CL

ANNE
GOODRICH

HIDSALL
DR 12

STREET

NOVER

STABLES

BAY TREE

PRESTBURY
CEMETERY

BEECH
CL

NOVERTON
AV

NOVERTON

Prestbury

HIGH

DEEP ST

Whaddon

Oakley
Recreation
Ground

Wymans Brook

Government
Communication
Headquarters

Noverton

Battledown

Coltham
Fields

Battledown
Manor

Hewletts
Lower Farm

Reservoir

Reservoir

Oakley
Farm

Hewletts
Reservoir

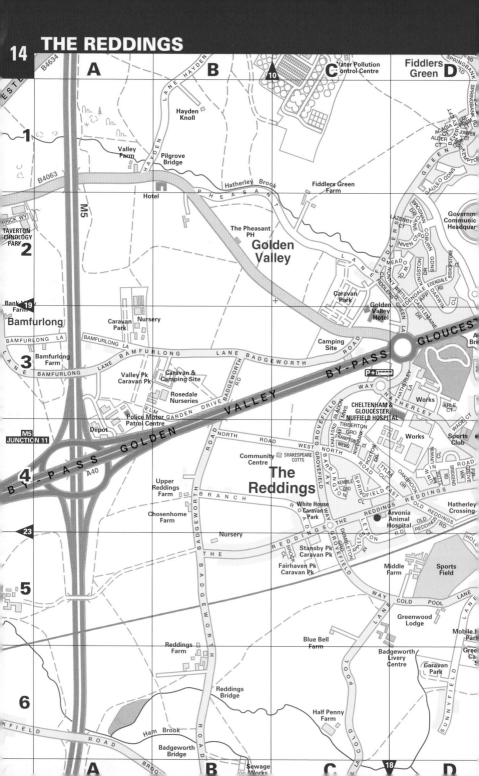

THE REDDINGS

A   B   C   Fiddlers Green   D

B4634
B4063

Hayden Knoll
Valley Farm
Pilgrove Bridge
HAYDEN LANE
Hatherley Brook
Hotel
PHEASANT
The Pheasant PH
Fiddlers Green Farm

Golden Valley

Caravan Park
Golden Valley Hotel

TAVERTON TECHNOLOGY PARK
RRICK WY
M5

Bank Farm
Bamfurlong
Caravan Park
Nursery
BAMFURLONG LA
Bamfurlong Farm
BAMFURLONG LANE
BAMFURLONG LANE BADGEWORTH
Camping Site

ROAD
BY-PASS
GLOUCEST

Valley Pk Caravan Pk
Caravan & Camping Site
ELM GARDEN DRIVE
Rosedale Nurseries
Police Motor Patrol Centre
Depot

M5 JUNCTION 11
A40
GOLDEN VALLEY BY-PASS

HATHERLEY WAY
Works
ARLE CT
WADE CT

CHELTENHAM & GLOUCESTER NUFFIELD HOSPITAL
Works
Sports Club

Upper Reddings Farm
BRANCH
NORTH ROAD
Community Centre
SHAKESPEARE COTTS
WEST NORTH

The Reddings

Chosenhome Farm
Nursery
BADGEWORTH RD
GROVEFIELD WAY
White House Caravan Park
Arvonia Animal Hospital
Hatherley Crossing
OLD REDDINGS RD

THE REDDINGS
Stansby Pk Caravan Pk
Fairhaven Pk Caravan Pk
Middle Farm
Sports Field

Reddings Farm
Blue Bell Farm
COLD POOL LANE
Greenwood Lodge
Mobile Pa
Gree Ca

Badgeworth Livery Centre
Caravan Park

Reddings Bridge
Half Penny Farm
SUNNYFIELD

KFIELD ROAD
Ham Brook
Badgeworth Bridge
Sewage Works

A   B   C   D

Coltham Elds

Moat

Green Acres Farm

School

Playing Field

Cricket Ground

Greenway Cottage

Battledown Manor 13

Glenfall House

Glenfall Farm

WADLEY COTTS

NATTON COTTS

ORCHARD COTTS

Ham Farm

Clinic

HOME FM CT

ASHLEY CLOSE

Ryeworth

Ham Brook

Ham

Ham Villa Farm

Sch

Charlton Kings

BRIARBANK RISE

Nazareth Ho

CASTLEFIELDS

River Chelt

Detmore House

Wellinghill House

East End

PEEL CT

Pol Sta

WAGERS CL

BALCARRAS

Schools

WOODGATE

BALCARRAS GDNS

Balcarras Farm

Cemetery

Playing Field

Playing Field

Little Herberts

Coxhorne Farm

CHARLTON KINGS IND EST

Cheltenham Park Hotel

Timbercombe Farm

Ashgrove Farm

Lilley Brook Golf Course

Club House

Timbercombe

Lilley Grove

Goss Covert

Jennings Grove

California Farm

SHURDINGTON

Chargrove

CHARGROVE BUSINESS CENTRE

Shurdington

Cricket Ground

South Park

Greatfield Farm

Brickhouse Farm

Oak Farm

The Oaklands

Church Farm

Playing Field

Comm Centre

Shurdington Bridge

Tynings Farm

Poultry Houses

LITTLE HILLS COTTS

Dutch Farm

Bickford House

Lynfield Farm

Crippetts Farm

Common Furze Farm

Nurseries

Brizen Farm

Shurdington Grove

Shurdington House Stables

Cowley Farm

Shurdington C of E Primary School

Sunfield Farm

White House

Gables Farm

Badgeworth Nurseries

Gloucestershire Wy

Ham Brook

Pit (disused)

Leckhampton FARM LANE

SHURDINGTON ROAD

LECKHAMPTON

A46

Ham Brook

Gold Pool La

Cole

Badgeworth

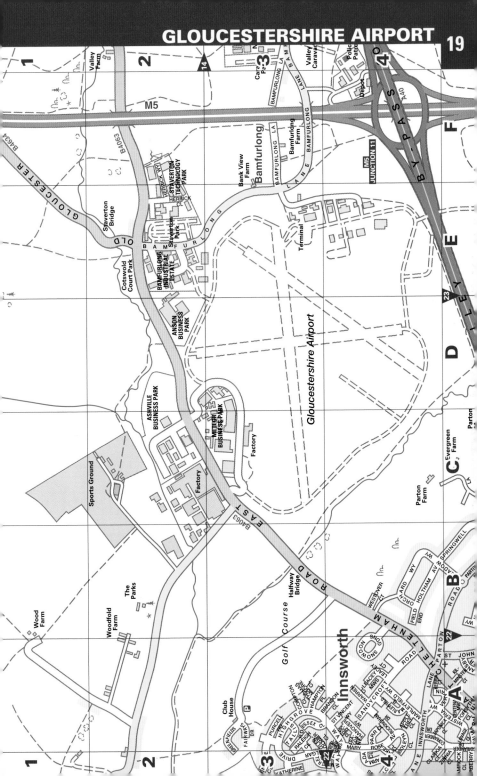

1
2
3
4

Valley Farm

M5

B4063

14

Care Pa

Valley Caravan

Police Patro

Depot

BAMFURLONG LANE

A40

BY-PASS

F

Bamfurlong

BAMFURLONG LA

Bamfurlong Farm

BAMFURLONG LANE

Bank View Farm

HERRICK WY

STAVERTON TECHNOLOGY PARK

HERRICK CL

OLD

Staverton Bridge

GLOUCESTER

ROAD

BAMFURLONG

Staverton Park

M5 JUNCTION 11

Terminal

E

Cotswold Court Park

BAMFURLONG INDUSTRIAL ESTATE

FURLONG

ANSON BUSINESS PARK

Gloucestershire Airport

23

D

ASHVILLE BUSINESS PARK

METEOR BUSINESS PARK

Factory

C

Evergreen Farm

LA

Parton

Parton Farm

Sports Ground

Factory

B4063

EAST

The Parks

Wood Farm

Woodfold Farm

ROAD

Halfway Bridge

Golf Course

CHELTENHAM

WESTOVER

ORCHARD WY

HOLTHAM AV

FIELD END

SPRINGWELL

ROAD PARTON

WY

B

Innsworth

ROAD

22

A

Club House

P

Parking

FAIRWAYS DR

GREENFIELDS

PURCELL

HIGH GROVE

FALKNER

ESSEX CL

RALEIGH

EDGAR DRIVE

HAMPTON

LEACROFT

ST VINCENT

ROSE

MARY

ST JOHN

LANE

CLOUCESTER ROAD

1
2
3
4

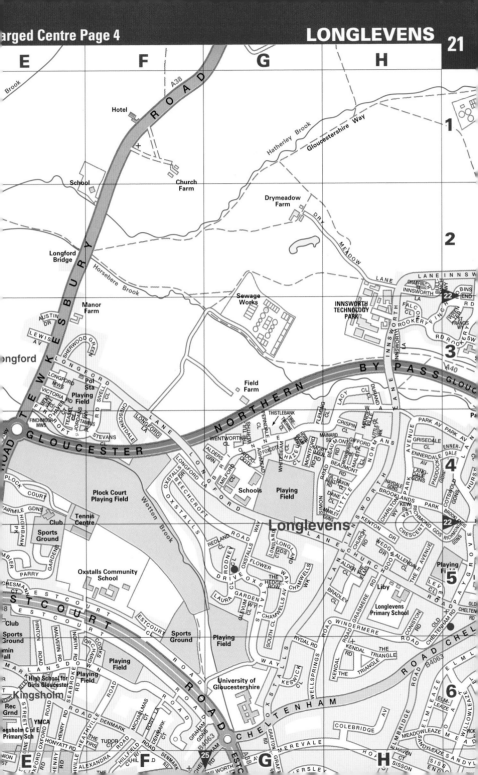

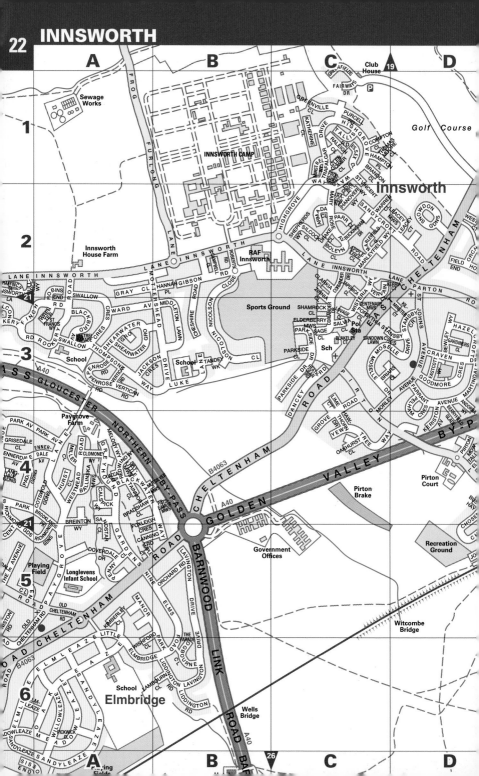

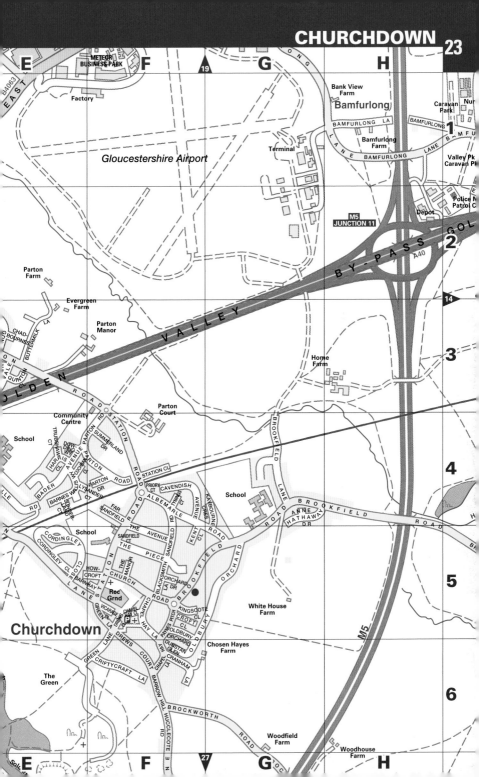

E F G H

META BUSINESS PARK

Bank View Farm

Bamfurlong

Caravan Park Nur

Factory

BAMFURLONG LA

BAMFURLONG

1

Gloucestershire Airport

Terminal

Bamfurlong Farm

BAMFURLONG LANE

BAMFURLONG

Valley Pk Caravan Pl

M5 JUNCTION 11

Police N Patrol C

Depot

BY-PASS

A40

GOL

2

14

Parton Farm

Evergreen Farm

VALLEY

Home Farm

3

BUTTERMILK LA

CHAD-BOURNE

Parton Manor

JLDEN

QUINTON

VALLEY

ROAD

Parton Court

Community Centre

STATION DR

SUMMERLAND

School

School

BROOKFIELD LANE

4

TRUSHAM CT

HARRIS CT

DOWTY WY

SCORAH

PARTON AVENUE

BARTON DR

SYLVANDER

STATION ROAD

PRIORY CT

CAVENDISH

ALBEMARLE

TINNINGS CT

KAYBOURNE CRES

School

BROOKFIELD

ROAD

BADER RD

BARNES WY

STIFF CL

FAR SANDFIELD

STATION CL

KENT CL

KAYBOURNE ROAD

BROOKFIELD ROAD

ANNE HATHAWAY DR

School

CORDINGLEY CL

COOMBE

BARHAY

GREEN LA

THE SANDFIELD CT

THE AVENUE

THE PIECE

SANDFIELD RD

ORCHARD

5

CORDINGLEY CL

HOW-CROFT

CHURCH

MANOR DR

BLACKSMITH

ORCHARD

BROOKFIELD ROAD

ORCHARD

Rec Grnd

VICARAGE

CHAPEL HAY CL

KINGSCOTE

White House Farm

Churchdown

CHURCH ROAD

CHAPEL HAY LA

PITCH CL

OLDBURY

ORCHARD

DUNSTAN GLEN

Chosen Hayes Farm

6

GREEN LANE

DREWS COURT

CRIFTYCROFT LA

BARROW HILL

CHAPEL LA

CRANHAM

The Green

HUCCLECOTE RD

BROCKWORTH

Woodfield Farm

Woodhouse Farm

ROAD

E F G H

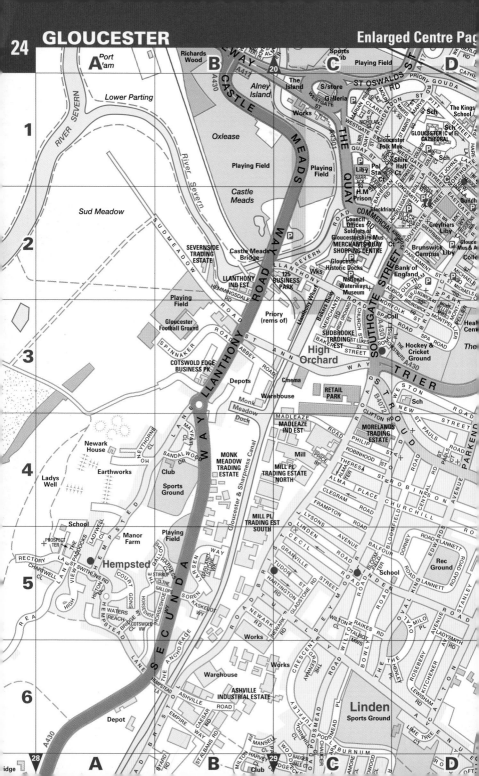

A
B
C
D
1
2
3
4
5
6
22
25
31
Playing Fields
Works
Wks
Factory
Sports Ground
THE LUTHER CHALLIS BSNS CENTRE
IMPERIAL GATE BUSINESS PARK
Hotel
Leisure Park
Zoons Court
CORINIUM AVENUE
BARNWOOD LINK RD
BARNWOOD ROAD
A40
A417
METEOR CT
Playing Field
Superstore
Offices
C & G
Warehouses
Depot
Factory
Barnwood
Nuclear Electric Office
School
Barnwood Park
Wotton Brook
Horsbere Brook
Pitt Mill
Youth Centre
Pol Sta
Liby
Hucclecote
Playing Field
Holly Ho
Abbeymead
Hucclecote Green
Bowling Green
M5
SANDYLEAZE
SISSON END
SISSON RD
SISSON ROAD
PICKWICK CLO
SAW MILLS END
FAIRWATER PK
GROVE CRESCENT
COLIN ROAD
BARNWOOD AV
LICHFIELD RD
JULIAN CL
BARNETT WAY
CREST WAY
LEY CT
BRIGHOUSE CT
WELVELAND LA
WOTTON CT
KEVIN CL
GROVELANDS
CHERSTON CT
WEIR BRIDGE CL
MANOR GDS
CASTLE COTTS
HUCCLECOTE ROAD
CREDON RD
KINGSTONE AV
DUNCROFT RD
KENNEDY CL
INSLEY GDNS
LANGTON CL
HINSLEY
GILPIN
GATTON WAY
BARNACRE DR
COLWELL AVENUE
BARRINGTON DR
ST MARGARETS RD
ELLESMERE CL
MAYFIELD DRIVE
HILLVIEW DRIVE
FIRCROFT CL
BURLEIGH CROFT
SILVERDALE PARADE
QUEENS CL
ST PHILLIPS CL
WILKES
CHERRY GDNS
DEER PARK RD
ZOONS RD
PITT MILL GDNS
MILLFIELDS
HORSEBERE ROAD
HAVELOCK RD
NOAKE RD
TYNDALE RD
CONWAY
CAMBERLEY CL
LAYNES ROAD
MOGRIDGE CL
NOTLEY PL
BRENSHAM CT
HOWARD PL
COXMORE CL
COPPICE MWS
BILLBROOK RD
COUSLEY CL
CARRISBROOKE
CHURCH ROAD
CHURCHVIEW DR
TOWER CL
SPIRE WAY
STEEPLE CL
TEMPLE CL
BELFRY
BROADSTONE CL
NEWSTEAD RD
WOODEND CL
LYNG CL
WOODGATE CL
LILLIESFIELD AVENUE
PINE TREE DR
UPTON LANE
UPTON CLOSE
FOXWELL DR
JENNER CL
PORCHESTER RD
SPENCER CL
INGLEWELL ROAD
FIELDCOTE DRIVE
ERMINSTER DR
GLENVILLE PDE
PINEMOUNT RD
MILLBRIDGE RD
KINGSCROFT RD
ELMGROVE
LYNTON ROAD
LYNMOUTH ROAD
SIMMONS RD
TREVOR ROAD
PARKWOOD CRES
ASHWOOD WAY
OAKWOOD DR
BRAMLEY MWS
GREEN WAY
APPLETON WAY
THE ORCHARDS
ORCHARD PK
LAXTON RD
RIPPIN CL
COXS WAY
ELLISON CL
DISCOVERY RD
GREIVE RD
JAMES CL
HOWGATE CL
MARTEN CL
OTTER RD
FOX CL
BROOKFIELD AVENUE
AMBROOK CRES
ST LAWRENCE RD
CONEY HILL RD
CASTLETON RD
SNOWSHILL CL
BROAD LEYS ROAD
METZ WAY
ABBEYMEAD AVENUE
STOWELL MWS
DODINGTON CL
SPINNEY RD
COPSE
THE DELL
MAREFIELD CL
GRASBY CL
THE HOLT
WHITEWELL CL
STONE CL
THE ORANGERY
THE THIRD
PINERY
NORTH
QUAIL CL
HARLEYS FLD
MIDDLE CFT
HAYWARD CL
WINDMILL FLD
SEVEN ACRES
GREAT GROVE
TRYGROVE
WEST LODGE DRIVE
PRICES GRND
YOUNGS ORCHARD
CLOVER PIECE
BLAKE HILL
MICKLE MEAD
STONEBRACK PIECE
DANCERS HILL
THE LARCHES
THE OAKS
THE HAZELS
THE MAPLES
ASHMEAD
STONEY BRIDGE
CARWARDINE FIELD
CLAUDIANS CL
VALERIAN CL
HADRIANS WY
ROMAN ROAD
CENTURION
SPARTAN CL
FOSSE CL
TRIBUNE PL
TRAJAN CL
MINERVA CL
VULCAN WY
JUPITER WY
MERCURY WY
NEPTUNE CL
SATURN CL
AUGUSTINE WAY
DIANAS CL
REMUS CL
CHOIRS CL
BISHOPS RD
PILGRIM CL
LADY CHAPEL RD
MINSTER GDNS
HENRY RYDER CL
PRIORY
ABBOTS ROAD
TRINITY RD
BAPTIST CL
FORBES CL
KIMBERLAND WY
PLANTATION
FRIARY RD
WIGMORE CL
MORWENT CL
THOMAS STOCK GDNS
BODENHAM FIELD
CROCK MEAD
THE MALVERNS
HAREBELL PL
HONEYSUCKLE DR
CORNFLOWER RD
FODIL
HOME GRND
FOXGLOVE CL
WOODBINE CL
SPEEDWELL
CHESTNUT
VERBENA CL
SNOWDROP CL
MEADOWSWEET
CHACELEY CL
BROADWELL CL
MEAD RD
LOBLEYS DR
HUNTLEY CL
CHERRINGTON
BRIERLEY CL
HORSLEY
KINGSCOTE
SUDGROVE
BROME RD
MARRAMS
VERNAL CL
MARJORAM CL
CAMOMILE CL
BORAGE CL
ANGELICA WY
THYME CL
TREE
TANSY CL
FALDO CL
COTTON CL
PALMER AV
CALDERDALE
DESFORD
LONGVILLE CL
HOMESTEAD
BITTERN AVENUE
HAWK CL
OSPREY CL
OWL CL
FIELDFARE
SWIFT RD
WOODCOCK
THRUSH CL
ORIOLE WY
THE CHASE
GREBE
School

Works

E F A G H

26

M5

1

HURRICANE

HURRICANE

32

CE

2

Commelines
Mill Farm

Home
Farm

Bondend

Bowden Hall
Hotel

Nut Hill

NUT HILL

NUT HILL

3

School

Bondend

Upton
Mill

Hall

**Upton
St. Leonards**

Whitley
Court

4

Poole's
Farm

STANLEY
WK

STANLEY
WK

Lake
House

Peaked
Acres

Moorend
Equestrian
Centre

Manor
Farm

VALLEY LANE

Portway
Farm

Gastrells
Farm

Prinknash
Abbey

5

Hardwicke
Farm

Moorend
Farm

PORTWAY

Ree's
Farm

Moorend

Pottery

*Prinknash
Park*

6

Prinknash
Park

E F G H

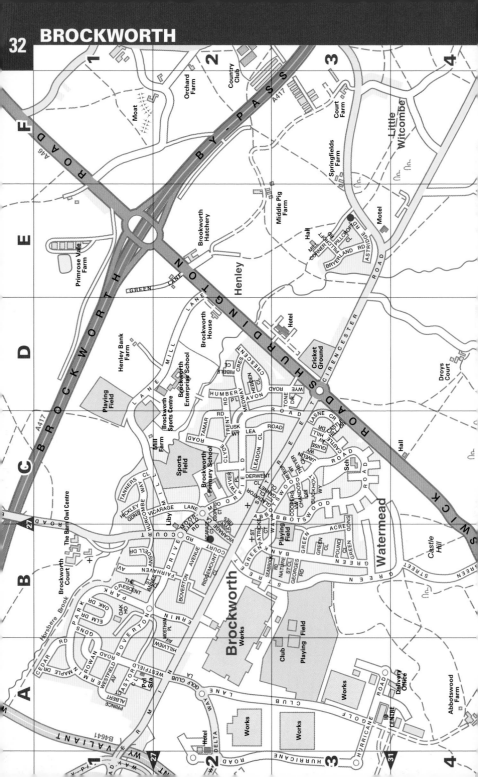

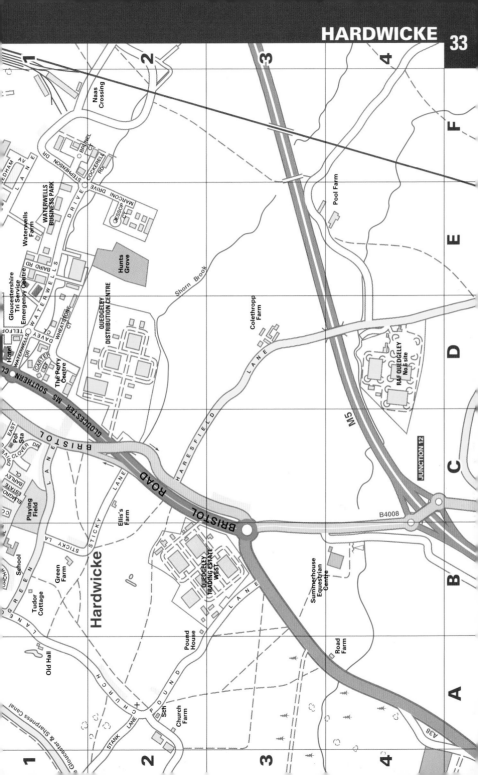

Naas Crossing

WATERWELLS BUSINESS PARK

Waterwells Farm

Gloucestershire Tri Service Emergency Centre

Hotel

The Parry Centre

QUEDGELEY DISTRIBUTION CENTRE

Hunts Grove

Shorn Brook

Colethrop Farm

Pool Farm

RAF QUEDGELEY No.6 site

GLOUCESTER M5 SOUTHERN

BRISTOL

BRISTOL ROAD

HARESFIELD LANE

M5

JUNCTION 12

B4008

Pol Sta

Playing Field

School

Green Farm

Tudor Cottage

Hardwicke

Ellis's Farm

Summerhouse Equestrian Centre

Road Farm

QUEDGELEY TRADING ESTATE WEST

Pound House

Old Hall

Church Farm

Sch

Gloucester & Sharpness Canal

STANK LANE

STICKY LA

GREEN LANE

CHURCH LANE

POUND LANE

LANE

A38

1 2 3 4

F E D C B A

1 2 3 4

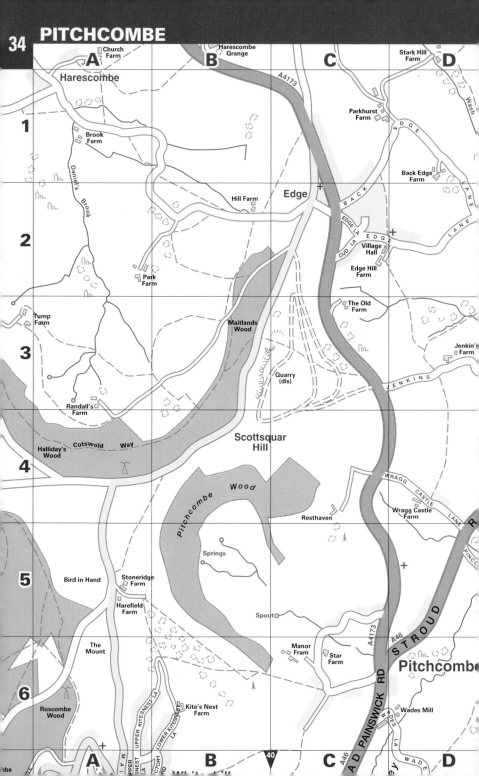

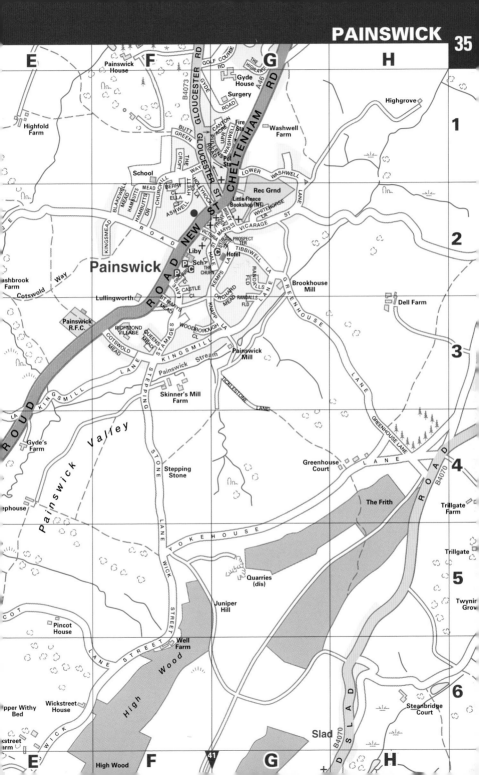

E   **F**   **G**   **H**

Painswick House

Highfold Farm

B4073

GLOUCESTER RD

GOLF COURSE

GYDE RD

THE HIGHLAND

A46

CHELTENHAM RD

Gyde House

Surgery

Highgrove

1

Washwell Farm

Fire Sta

School

THE CROFT

BLACKWELL MEAD

HAMBUTTS MEAD

HAMBUTTS DR

CHURCH HILL

ROAD

KINGSMEAD

CANTON ACRE

PULLENS RD

UPPER WASHWELL

Pot Sta

LOWER WASHWELL LANE

Rec Grnd

WHITEHORSE ST

VICARAGE

2

Painswick

ROAD

NEW ST

ST MARYS ST

HOLLYHOCK LANE

ELLA

ASHWELL

Little Fleece Bookshop (NT)

VICTORIA ST

ST MARYS ST

BISLEY ST

ST MARYS

Liby

Sch

C

P

P

Hotel

THE CHURN

KEMPS

PROSPECT TER

TIBBIWELL LA

ORCHARD MEAD

RANDALLS FLD

RANDALLS FLD

Brookhouse Mill

Dell Farm

3

Ashbrook Farm

Cotswold Way

Lullingworth

Painswick R.F.C.

RICHMOND VILLAGE

COTSWOLD MEAD

QUEENS MEAD

ST MARYS MEAD

KINGSMILL LANE

ST JAMES

CASTLE CL

WHARF LA

Woodborough CL

Painswick Mill

GREENHOUSE LANE

Painswick Stream

Skinner's Mill Farm

STEPPING STONE LANE

TICKLESTONE LANE

LANE

GREENHOUSE LANE

Greenhouse Court

4

Gyde's Farm

KINGSMILL LANE

Painswick Valley

ROAD

ephouse

Stepping Stone

YOKEHOUSE LANE

The Frith

B4070 ROAD

Trillgate Farm

Trillgate

Twynir Grov

5

COT

Pincot House

WICK STREET LANE

Quarries (dis)

Juniper Hill

Steanbridge Court

6

pper Withy Bed

Wickstreet House

ckstreet Farm

High Wood

Well Farm

High Wood

Slad

B4070 D SLAD

E   **F**   **G**   **H**

High Wood

41

A **B** **C** **D**

1

Square
Covert

PASSAGE ROAD

MOOR ST

STREET

CHURCH

Saul
Sch

Saul
Farm

Locks

Junction
Bridge

Cotswold Canals Trust
Heritage Centre
C

River Frome

Whitminster
House

2

HIGH

Malthouse
Farm

Sandfield
Bridge

Grain
Store

Sandfield
Mill

LANE

LANE

Oatfield

Walk
Bridge

Weir

Whitminster
Bridge

Dunstalls

B4071

BRIDGE

3

Saul
Lodge

FRAMPTON
ON SEVERN
IND PK

LAKE LANE

THE OVAL

THE OVAL APP

School

Comm
Centre

ANN WICKS RD

PHILLIMORE GDS

OATFIELD RD

RD

Surgery

WHITMINSTER

Recreation
Ground

Police
House

Frampton on Severn

ROAD

PERRY

Cricket
Green

4

Severn Way

Manor
Farm

Farm
Pool

The Green

Frampton
Court

Works

Nether
Cove

The Gloucester and Sharpness Canal

5

Village
Hall

STREET

WATERY

WHITTLES LA

LANE

Townfield
Farm

W

6

CHURCH LA

SCHOOL
ROW

VICARAGE

THE

The Old
Vicarage
Res. Home

GLEBE CL

MEADOW
VW

Denfurlong
Farm

MARSH LA

Park Corner
Cottage

Nastfield
Farm

A **B** **C** **D**

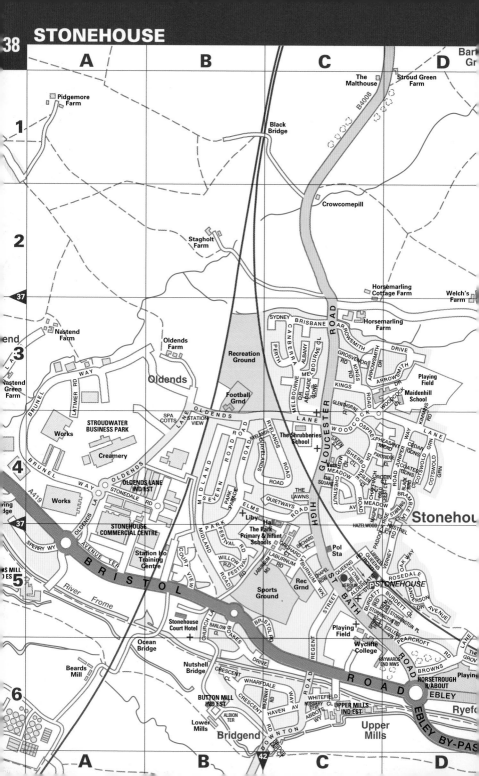

Bar
Gr

A **B** **C** **D**

1

Pidgemore Farm

The Malthouse

Stroud Green Farm

B4008

Black Bridge

Crowcomepill

2

Stagholt Farm

Horsemarling Cottage Farm

Welch's Farm

37

Nastend Farm

Horsemarling Farm

SYDNEY

BRISBANE

3

Nastend Green Farm

Oldends Farm

Recreation Ground

GROSVENOR RD

ARROWSMITH

ARROWSMITH DRIVE

Playing Field

Oldends

WAY

LATIMER RD

BRUNEL

SPA COTTS

OLDENDS LANE

STATION VIEW

Football Grnd

CANBERRA

PERTH

MELBOURNE

ADELAIDE GDNS

ALBANY

MELBOURNE GDNS

BOURNE CL

KINGS RD

KINGS

GLENTHORNE CL

GLOUCESTER ROAD

ARROWSMITH

WOODCOCK

KIMMINS RD

Maidenhill School

STROUDWATER BUSINESS PARK

Works

Creamery

OLDENDS LANE IND EST

STONEDALE RD

MIDLAND ROAD

SEVERN ROAD

RYELANDS ROAD

RYELANDS

The Shrubberies School

WOODCOCK

OSPREY

GREEN

SHERBORNE DR

YEW TREE MEAD

PHEASANT MEAD

PARTRIDGE

CEDAR GDNS

JUNIPER CL

COATES GDNS

BLACK THORN

BRAMBLE

COTSWOLD GRN

COTSWOLD

BRUNEL

WAY

4

Works

OLDENDS LA

STONEHOUSE COMMERCIAL CENTRE

Station Ho Training Centre

PARK PARADE

FESTIVAL RD

MIDLAND

PARK

ELMS

QUIETWAYS

THE LAWNS

ROAD

THE SQUARE

SHERBORNE DR

ROBIN

CHESTNUT

MAGPIE

RISE

KESTREL

BRAMBLE

STIRLING

Stonehou

HAZELWOOD

A419

37

SPERRY WY

BRISTOL

AVENUE TER

COURT VIEW

WILLOW RD

FESTIVAL RD

LABURNUM

LABURNUM

ORCHARD

ORCHARD

CHAPEL ST

QUEENS

QUEENS

PADDOCK RISE

OAK WAY

ROSEDALE

5

River Frome

Stonehouse Court Hotel

BARLOW CL

CHURCH LA

OAKES CL

BRISTOL RD

DRIVE

REGENT

The Park Primary & Infant Schools

Liby Hall

Sports Ground

Rec Grnd

Pol Sta

VERDUN

QUEENS

ALDERGATE

BURDETT

BURDETT RD

STORMONT RD

STORRINGTON RD

COLLEGE

STONEHOUSE

BATH ROAD

ANDERSON AVENUE

PEARCROFT RD

BROWNS

THE GROV

Playin

S MILL ES

ng dge

Ocean Bridge

Beards Mill

Nutshell Bridge

CRESCENT CL

WHARFDALE

HAVEN AV

CRESCENT

ALBION TER

MEADOW

DOWNTON

WAY

WHITEFIELD

NURSERY TER

ABBOTS WY

Playing Field

Wycliffe College

HAYWARDS END MWS

HORSETROUGH R/ABOUT

EBLEY

Ryef

6

Lower Mills

BUTTON MILL IND EST

Bridgend

42

UPPER MILLS IND EST

Upper Mills

EBLEY ROAD

EBLEY BY-PAS

A **B** **C** **D**

E **F** **G** **H**

Ruscombe Wood

Ruscombe

1

Randwick Wood

Lightwood Lane

Light Wood

Ludle Gree

Cross Dyke

Long Barrow

Standish Quarry (disused)

Castle Quarry (disused)

THE STOCKS

Randwick

THE BUNGALOWS

EPWORTH MNT

Ocker Hill

Ruscon Farm

2

The Ash

A 5 H

School

Springs

LANE

Hall

Ruscombe Road

40

Hill Farm

Cotswold Way

Maiden Hill

LANE

THE RYELANDS

Court Farm

Playing Field

3

The Fuzzies

SANDPITS

Sandpits

Maiden Hill House

FAR

Westrip

WESTRIP

RIDGE

LANE

REDHOUSE LANE

THE

WESTRIP LANE

HUNTERS

FOX

PERRY ORCHARD

HAWTHORN RISE

THE MARTINS

WORDENS

THE MARTINS

THE HENLEY CT

LANE

DEVONAS

SPRINGFIELD

ST MICHAELS RD

ETHELDENE

GREEN RD

HILLCREST

MOOR HALL CASHES

HUMPHREYS

PARK

Rec Grnd

Cashes Green School

HARPERFIELD

COTSWOLD

PARK

DRIVE

ROAD

Townsend

Humphreys End

ACRE PL

END

Sprs

Puckshole

PRINCES RD

MOOR HALL PL

MOSELEY RD

STANTON

MILL FARM DRIVE

Little Mill Farm

WALTER PRESTON CT

MARLING

MILL FA

CRES

Park Farm

Archw Scho

Play Fie

Par En

40

4

Doverow Hill

Cotswold Way

The Croft Farm

GLYNFIELD

FOXMOOR LANE

THE BASSETS

THE BRIDLE

THE BASSETS

HUNTERS CL

Cashes Green

THE STIRRUP

QUEENS ROAD

SPINNING WHEEL CL

MOSELEY RD

CRESSY

KINGLEY

MALVERN GDNS

HYETT

CASHES GREEN ROAD

Hamwell Leaze

Amb

Fire Sta

5

Springs

Oaks

DEVEREAUX CRES

DEVEREAUX RD

ROBBINS

DEVEREAUX CRES

FOXMOOR RISE

THE BEAGLES

BERKELEY CL

WAY

BEAGLES

THE

UPPER CHURCH RD

Sch

WHITEHOUSE RD

ASHWAY

HILLY FORT VW

ROAD

PAGAN

BRIDGE

Grove arm

EAST VW

SOUTH VW

ELM TER

Foxmoor County Primary School

DR

SCH TER

HUNTINGDON CL

CEDAR CL

CHAPEL LANE

WESTWARD CT

Victory Park

ST MATTHEWS CT

CHURCH

MONKEY PUZZLE

FROME GDNS

Supermkt B4008

ROAD

S/mkt

HILLY FORT VW

BRADFIELD RD

BLAFIELD RD

SO

DUDBRIDGE

SELSLEY RD

6

LEY

MERTON CL

ROAD

ORCHARD RD

ORCHARD

ORCHARD RD

WESTWARD ROAD

BRIDGE RD

Ebley

THE GROVE

HOME ORCHARD

HOLLY TREE GDNS

BRIDGE

ORCHARD MEAD

Cotswold Indoor Bowls Club

MEADOW LA

WEST

Stroudwater Canal (disused) Locks

RYEFORD SAW MILLS IND EST

A419

Refuse Tip

Council Offices

E **F** **43** **G** *Frome* **H** **S**

PAH S

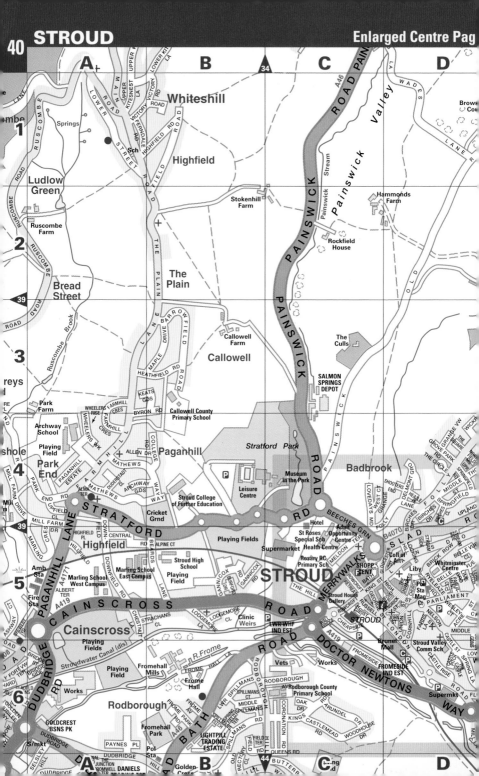

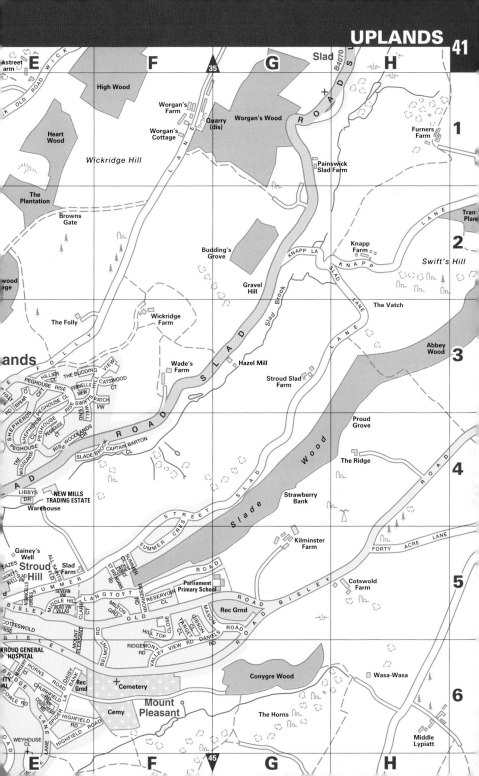

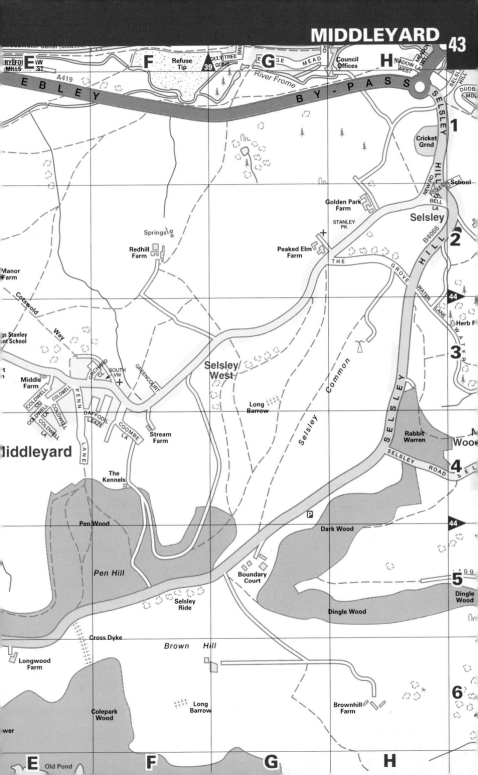

E — Coldwater Canal (disused)
RYEFOI MILLS · W ST
A419

F — Refuse Tip · HOLLY TREE GDNS · 39

G — BRI · EDGE MEAD · River Frome · Council Offices

H — MEADOW LA WEST · SELSEY HILL · DUDB MDW

BY-PASS

EBLEY

SELSLEY HILL

1
Cricket Grnd
NEW RD · FOLLEY LA · BELL LA
School

Golden Park Farm
STANLEY PK
Selsley

Springs

Redhill Farm

Peaked Elm Farm

B4066

2
THE GROVE
WATER LANE
44
Herb F

Manor Farm

Cotswold Way

3
Common
W A T E R

js Stanley nt School

ORCHARD CL
SOUTH VW
GREENCOURT
PENN

Selsley West

Middle Farm
COLDWELL
COLDWELL CL
COLDWELL TCE
COLDWELL LA

DAFFODIL LEAZE
COOMBE LA

Stream Farm

Long Barrow

SELSLEY

Rabbit Warren
Woo

4
SELSLEY ROAD
SEL

Middleyard

PENN LANE

The Kennels

P

Dark Wood

44

Pen Wood

Boundary Court

Dingle Wood

5
Dingle Wood
AGG

Pen Hill

Selsley Ride

Cross Dyke

Brown Hill

6
Longwood Farm

Colepark Wood

Long Barrow

Brownhill Farm

wer

E — Old Pond

F

G

H

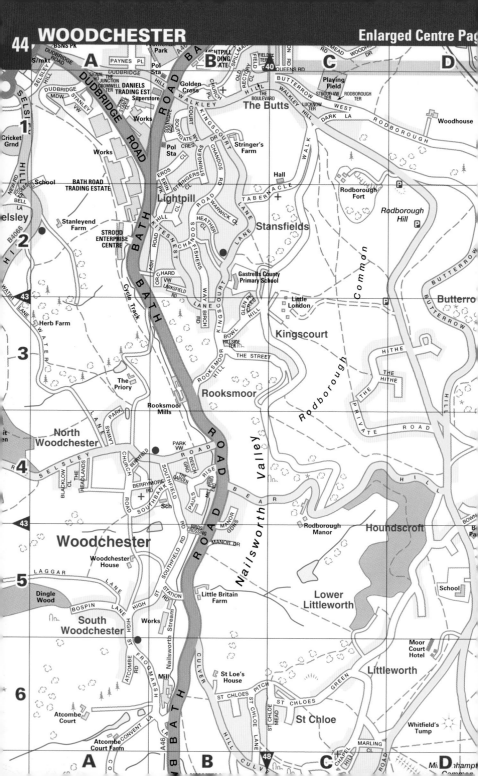

A B C D

BSNS PK
PAYNES PL
DUDBRIDGE ROAD
Brownhill Park
LIGHTPILL PADDING GATE
FIELD TER
WOODBUR DR
RD MEAD

DUDBRIDGE ROAD
S/mkt
Pol Sta
OLD RECTORY
QUEENS RD
STROUD VW
RODBOROUGH TER

SIGNAL THE JUNCTION CROMWELL
DANIELS TRADING EST
Golden Cross
CHURCH LA
HILL
WALKLEY HILL
LUCKNOW TER
WEST RODBOROUGH

SELSLEY HILL
DUDBRIDGE MDW
STANLEY VW
Superstore
THE BOULEVARD
Playing Field
DARK LA
Woodhouse

1
Cricket Grnd
Works
WALKLEY COURT
KINGSCOURT DR
Stringer's Farm

DUDBRIDGE
Works
SOUTHGATE
CHANDOS RD
STRINGERS CL
Hall
Rodborough Fort

NEWND POOLES
Works
Pol Sta
CRES
EROS CL
TABERNACLE
Rodborough Hill

School
BATH ROAD TRADING ESTATE
Lightpill
WARWICK CT
Stansfields

BELL LA
elsley
Stanleyend Farm
STROUD ENTERPRISE CENTRE
HILL RD
HEATHER CL
ERIN PK
LANE
Little London

B4066
2
HILL
KITESNEST
WOODFISHERS
Gastrells County Primary School
Common

WATER
ORCHARD VW LARKSFIELD RD
BIRCH RD
GLEN PK HILL
Kingscourt

43
Herb Farm
Cycle Track
WAY
KINGSCOURT RD
BOWL LANE
HILLSIDE TER
THE STREET

3
LANE
The Priory
ROOKSMOOR HILL
Rooksmoor
Rodborough

Rooksmoor Mills
PARK SNWS
BATH ROAD
Nailsworth Valley
THE HITHE
THE PRIVATE ROAD

4
North Woodchester
SELSLOW
THE HEADLANDS
PARK VW
BEECH
GRO
BERRYMORE RD
BERRYFIELD
RISE
BEAR
HILL
BOWN

BLACKLOW CL
CHURCH RD
SOUTHFIELD RD
GARDEN
PAULS
MILL END
MANOR GDNS
Rodborough Manor
Houndscroft
B Pa

43
SOUTHBANK
Sch
BIRDS CROSSING
MANOR RD

Woodchester
LAGGAR
Woodchester House
SOUTHFIELD RD
STATION RD

5
LANE
Dingle Wood
BOSPIN LANE
HIGH ST
Little Britain Farm
Lower Littleworth
School

South Woodchester
Works
Nailsworth Stream
Moor Court Hotel

6
ATCOMBE
FROGMARSH
Mill
St Loe's House
CULVER
PITCH
GREEN
Littleworth

Atcombe Court
CONVENT LA
ST CHLOES
ST CHLOE MEAD
ST CHLOES
St Chloe
Whitfield's Tump

Atcombe Court Farm
BATH RD
A446
HILL
CULVER
CHAPEL
MARLING CL

A B **48** C D

E   **F**   **G**   **H**

Middle Lypiatt

The Limekilns

Dry Hill Wood

The Heavens

Bowbridge

Heavans Wood

Thrupp Farm

Nether Lypiatt Manor

Thrupp

Claypits Farm

Claypits Wood

Quarryhill Farm

Mackhouse Wood

GRIFFIN MILL ESTATE

Works

School

Beechgrove Farm

Park Wood

Lawrenceland Wood

Factory

Merlins Mill

Far Thrupp

Bagpath Farm

PHOENIX TRADING ESTATE

Stringer's Wood

Quarhouse Farm

Quarhouse

Thames and Severn Canal (dis)

CANAL IRONWORKS IND EST

Upper Bourne

Newlands Farm

Football Grnd

Greystones Farm

Brimscombe

Lower Bourne

CLARKES CL

Hillside Farm

Brimscombe Mill

PORT IND EST

GOLDEN VALLEY

Mill

COTSWOLD VALLEY CL

School

Brimscombe Farm

Wks

Wimberley Mills

Swellshill

School

Bourne Bridge

Jacobs Knowle

Cemy

Hotel

Knave-in-hole

Burleigh Farm

Burleigh Tower

Besbury Farm

E   **F**   **G**   **H**

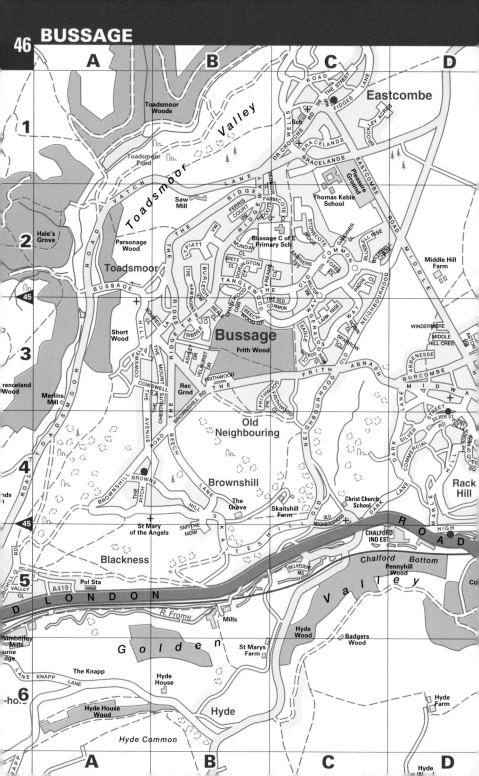

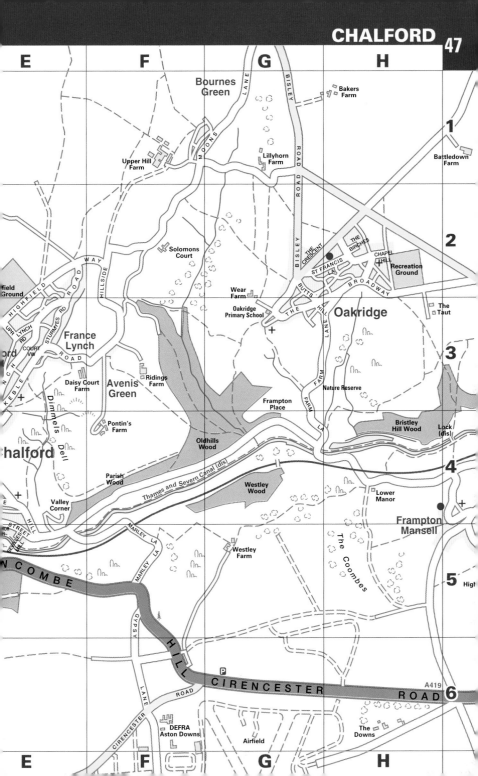

E   F   G   H

Bournes Green

Bakers Farm

MOONS LANE

BISLEY ROAD

Lillyhorn Farm

Upper Hill Farm

Battledown Farm

1

Solomons Court

THE BIRCHES

THE CRESCENT

CHAPEL HILL

ST FRANCIS LA

Recreation Ground

BROADWAY

2

field Ground

WAY

HIGHFIELD RD

HILLSIDE

STURMES RD

Wear Farm

Oakridge Primary School

THE BUTTS

Oakridge

The Taut

UPH LYNCH RD

ROAD

COURT VW

France Lynch

KEBLE

LA

Daisy Court Farm

Avenis Green

Ridings Farm

FARM LANE

Nature Reserve

3

ord

LYNCH

Dimmels Dell

Pontin's Farm

Frampton Place

Bristley Hill Wood

Lock (dis)

halford

Oldhills Wood

Thames and Severn Canal (dis)

4

Parish Wood

Westley Wood

Lower Manor

Frampton Mansell

Valley Corner

STREET HILL

BENNLESS ST

MARLEY LA

Westley Farm

The Coombes

5

High

NCOMBE

MARLEY LA

GYPSY

HILL

P

DEFRA Aston Downs

CIRENCESTER ROAD

A419

6

CIRENCESTER LANE

ROAD

Airfield

The Downs

E   F   G   H

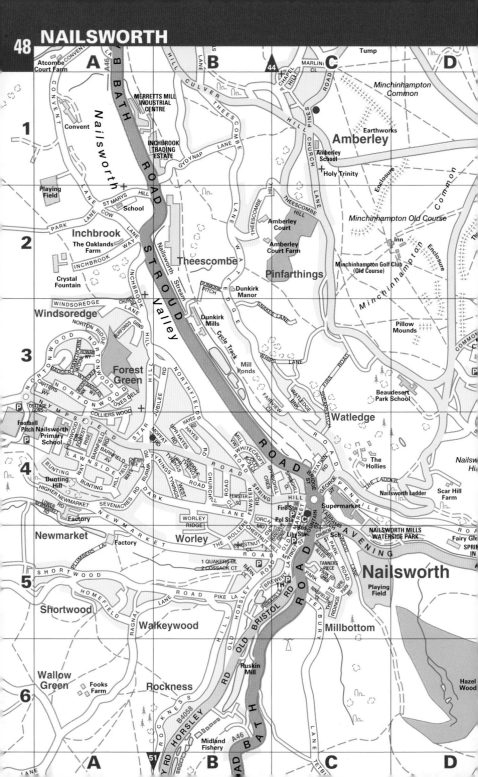

Map grid references (columns A–D, rows 1–6):

A
Atcombe Court Farm
Convent
Nailsworth
Playing Field
St Marys
School
COW LANE
Inchbrook
The Oaklands Farm
Crystal Fountain
WINDSOREDGE
Windsoredge
NORTON RIDGE
WOOD
BADGERS
ROWAN
CARTER'S
COTTAGE GDNS
Football Pitch Nailsworth Primary School
COLLIERS WOOD
Bunting Hill
HIGHER NEWMARKET
LOWER NEWMARKET RD
Factory
Newmarket
Factory
PLUMBERS LA
SHORTWOOD
HOMEFIELD
Shortwood
RAGNAL
Wallow Green
Fooks Farm

B
A46
BATH ROAD
MERRETTS MILL INDUSTRIAL CENTRE
CULVER HILL
THEESCOMBE
INCHBROOK TRADING ESTATE
GYDYNAP LANE
THEESCOMBE
Theescombe
Nailsworth Stream
DUNKIRK PITCH
Dunkirk Mills
STROUD VALLEY
Cycle Track
NORTHFIELDS RD
JUBILEE RD
STAR
HAYES
UPR HAYES RD
HAYES RD
MIDDLE HAYES
WEST TYNINGS
CHURCH LANE
MOFFAT RD
CHERRY TREE CL
BURMA
DARK
SEVENACRES RD
NEWMARKET
WORLEY RIDGE
Worley
THE ROLLERS
CHESTNUT CL
1 QUAKERS CL
2 COSSACK CT
BARN
HORSLEY ROAD
PIKE LA
Walkeywood
RAGNAL
OLD HORSLEY HILL RD
B4058
Rockness
Midland Fishery
A46

C
Tump
MARLIN CL
CHAPEL HILL
44
PINES
MARLING
ROAD
HILLS
CHURCH
Amberley
Amberley School
Holy Trinity
THEESCOMBE
Amberley Court
Amberley Court Farm
Pinfarthings
Dunkirk Manor
SNAKES LANE
WHIBS LANE
FAIRVIEW RD
WATLEDGE BNK
FIRS ROAD
Mill Ponds
SPRATSBROOK
Watledge
The Hollies
George
Supermarket
STATION RD
BRIDGE
HILL
SPRINGHILL
SPRING CRES
FEWSTER SQ
WHITECROFT RD
Fire Sta
Pol Sta
Bus Sta
Liby Sta
ORCH MD
BREWERY
Sch
ABRAMS PITCH
GROVE
TANNERS PIECE
PRIORY
RINGFIELD
THP
BRISTOL ROAD
OLD BRISTOL RD
Nailsworth
Playing Field
Millbottom
Ruskin Mill
BATH ROAD
PARK
TETBURY
CHESTNUT

D
Minchinhampton Common
Earthworks
Enclosure
Common
Minchinhampton Old Course
Inn
Minchinhampton Golf Club (Old Course)
Minchinhampton Common
Enclosure
Pillow Mounds
COMMON
Beaudesert Park School
Nailsw Hi
Scar Hill Farm
Nailsworth Ladder
THE LADDER
PENSILE
AVENING
NAILSWORTH MILLS WATERSIDE PARK
Fairy Gl
SPRI IN
Hazel Wood

ROAD, LANE markers
51

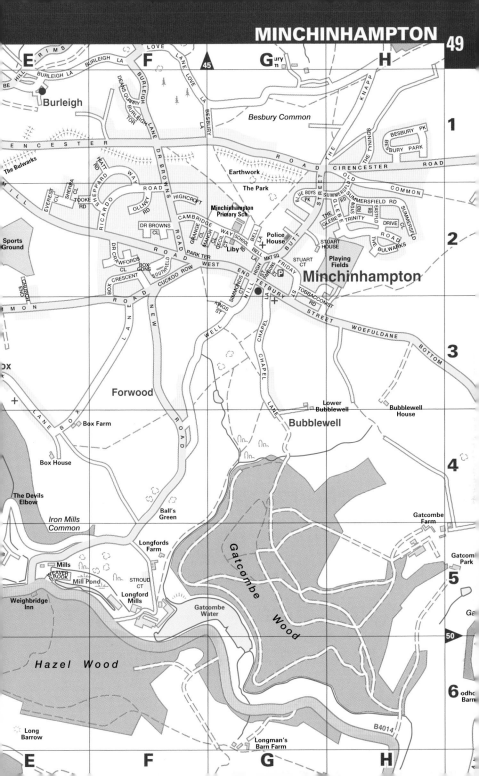

E **F** **45** **G** **H**

1

2

3

4

5

6

Burleigh

BURLEIGH LA
BE HILL
BURLEIGH LA
RIMS
HILL
LOVE LANE
LOVE LA
BESBURY LA
DEANS QUARRY
BURLEIGH LANE
TOR

Besbury Common

THE KNAPP

BESBURY PK
BESBURY PARK
THE TYNINGS

ENCESTER

The Bulwarks

CIRENCESTER ROAD

ROAD

Earthwork

The Park

OLD

COMMON

HIATT
SHEPPARD
EVEREST CL
SHERPA CL
TOOKE RD
RICARDO
WAY
OLLNE RD
DR BROWNS
HIGHCROFT
CAMBRIDGE
ROAD
DR BROWNS CL

Minchinhampton
Primary Sch

BLUE BOYS
PK

SUMMERSFI
SUMMERSFIELD RD
EASTFLD
THE GLEBE
SUMMERSFD
THE GLEBE
TRINITY
THE BULWARKS
DRIVE
SUMMERSFD
ROAD

STREET
BUTT

GRANGE CL
MANOR CL
CECIL CL
SCHOOL RD
BELL
BELL LA

Liby

Police
House

MKT SQ

STUART
HOUSE

PARSONS
FRIDAY

STUART
CT

PLAYING
Fields

Sports
Ground

DR CRAWFORDS CL
BOX
GDNS
CRESCENT
PARK TER
WEST
SOUTHFIELD
ROAD
CUCKOO ROW

HILL END

SIMMONDS
HIGH STREET

Minchinhampton

BOX ROAD

KINGS
ST

CHAPEL

WELL

TOBBACCONIST
RD

ENCESTER

COMMON

NEW
ROAD
LANEAD
BOX LANE

Forwood

CHAPEL LANE

Lower
Bubblewell

WOEFULDANE
BOTTOM

STREET

Bubblewell
House

Bubblewell

Box Farm

Box House

The Devils
Elbow

Iron Mills
Common

Ball's
Green

Longfords
Farm

Gatcombe
Farm

Gatcom
Park

5

Mills
WEAVERS BROOK
Mill Pond

Weighbridge
Inn

STROUD
CT

Longford
Mills

Gatcombe
Water

Gatcombe Wood

50

Hazel Wood

Ga

odho
Barn

Long
Barrow

B4014

Longman's
Barn Farm

E **F** **G** **H**

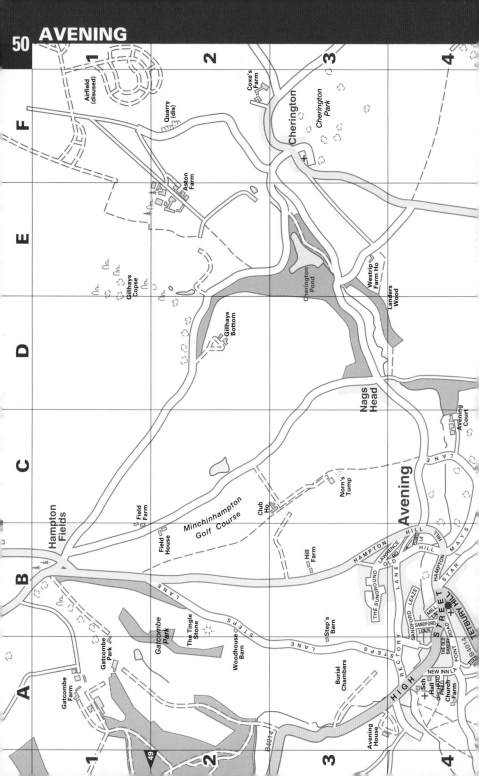

Airfield (disused)

Quarry (dis)

Coxe's Farm

Cherington

Cherington Park

Aston Farm

Gillhays Copse

Westrip Farm Ho

Cherington Pond

Landers Wood

Gillhays Bottom

Nags Head

Hampton Fields

Field Farm

Minchinhampton Golf Course

Club Ho

Field House

Norn's Tump

Avening

Gatcombe Park

The Tingle Stone

Hill Farm

HAMPTON

LAWRENCE

OLD RD

HILL

HILL

Avening Court

LANE

MAYS

TETBURY HILL

STREET

HAMPTON HILL

STAR

Gatcombe Park

Woodhouse Barn

Step's Barn

THE SUNGROUND

LANE

SANDFORD LEAZE

SANDFORD LEAZE

MILL

Gatcombe Farm

STEPS

LANE

RECTORY

Burial Chambers

STEPS

HIGH

NEW INN LA

Sch

Hall

ORCHARD

POINT ROAD

Church

Farm

B4014

Avening House

B4014

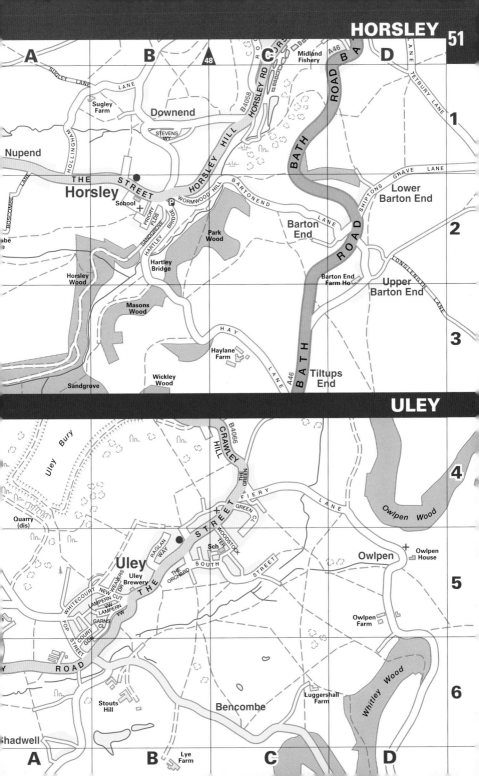

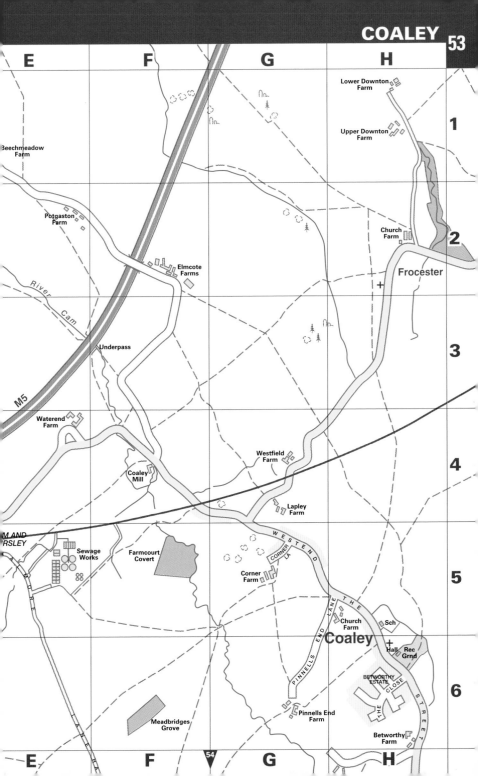

E   F   G   H

1

Lower Downton Farm

Upper Downton Farm

Beechmeadow Farm

Potgaston Farm

2

Church Farm

Frocester

Elmcote Farms

River Cam

Underpass

3

M5

Waterend Farm

Westfield Farm

4

Coaley Mill

Lapley Farm

M AND RSLEY

Sewage Works

Farmcourt Covert

WESTEND

CORNER LA

Corner Farm

5

PINNELLS END LANE

THE LANE

Church Farm

Sch

Coaley

Hall

Rec Grnd

BETWORTHY ESTATE

THE CLOSE

6

Meadbridges Grove

Pinnells End Farm

THE STREET

Betworthy Farm

E   F   G   H

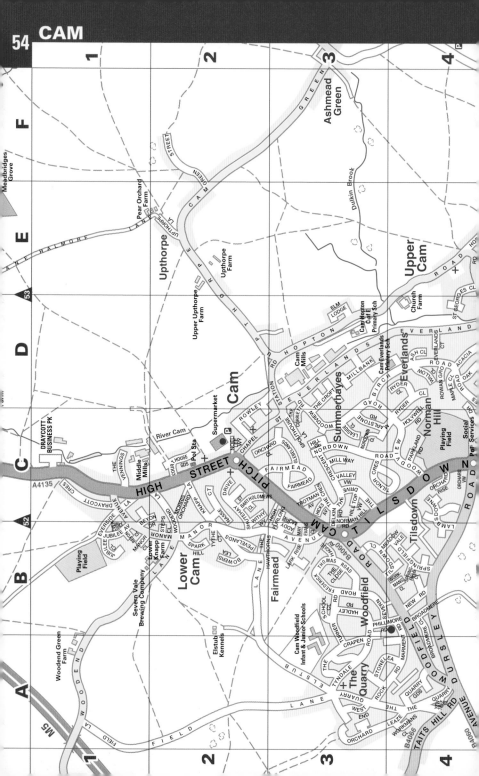

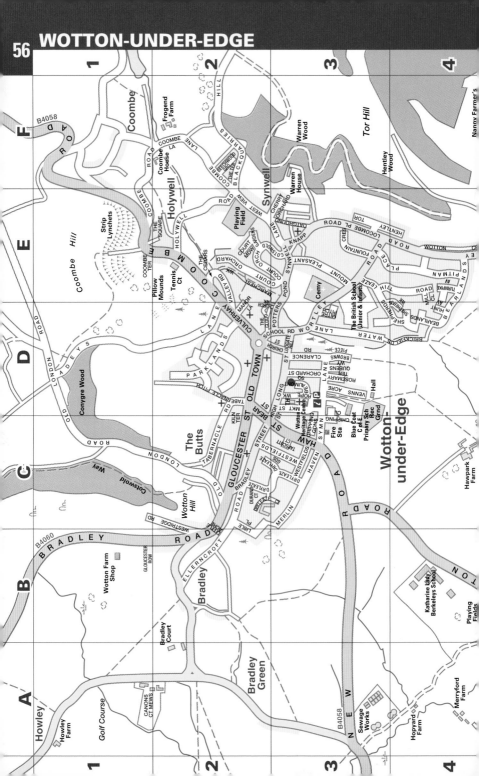

Howley

Coombe

Frogend Farm

Coombe House

Holwell

Tor Hill

Warren Wood

Hentley Wood

Synwell

Warren House

Nanny Farmer's

B4058 ROAD

Strip Lynchets

Coombe Hill

Pillow Mounds

Tennis Ct

The Cedars

Playing Field

The British School (Junior & Infants)

Cemy

Convigre Wood

Wotton Hill

The Butts

Cotswold Way

Wotton Farm Shop

GLOUCESTER ROW

OLD LONDON ROAD

Bradley

B4060 BRADLEY

Bradley Court

Bradley Green

Wotton Heritage Centre

Fire Sta

Blue Coat C of E Primary Sch

Rec Grnd

Hall

Hawpark Farm

Wotton-under-Edge

Katharine Lady Berkeleys School

Playing Fields

Howley Farm

Golf Course

CANONS CT MEWS

Sewage Works

Merryford Farm

Hopyard Farm

B4058

NEW ROAD

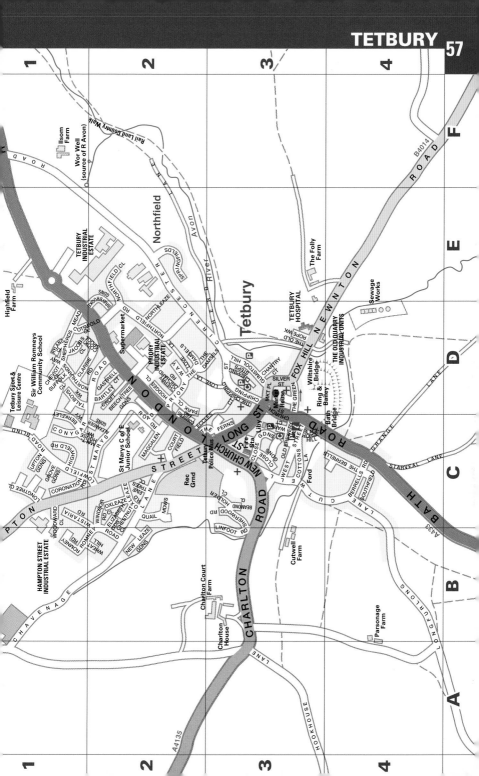

Map of Tetbury

Grid references: A B C D E F (columns), 1 2 3 4 (rows)

Ilsom Farm
Wor Well (source of R Avon)
Rail Land Country Walk
Northfield
River Avon
ROAD
B4014
ROAD
The Folly Farm
TETBURY HOSPITAL
Sewage Works
THE OLD QUARRY INDUSTRIAL UNITS
FOX HILL NEWTON
Wiltshire Ring & Bailey
Bath Bridge
CHANGE LANE
STARVEAL LANE
BATH ROAD
A433
LANE
THE BERRELLS
BERRELLS RD
SOUTHFIELD
THE CUT
LONGFURLONG
Parsonage Farm
Cutwell Farm
HOOKHOUSE LANE
A4135
CHARLTON ROAD
CHARLTON LANE
Charlton House
Charlton Court Farm
LINFOOT RD
BEAMOND CL
SHERWOOD RD
HOLKER CL
QUAIL
MDWS
Rec Grnd
Tetbury Police Mus
Fire Stn
Lby
CLOSE GDNS
OLD BREWERY
COTTONS STREET
WEST ST
THE CLOSE
FERNS
NEW CHURCH ROAD
LONG ST
NEW CHURCH ST
CHURCH STREET
THE GREEN
Mkt Pl
Mkt House
SILVER ST
CHANTRY
CT
CHIPPING STEPS
CUSTOM CL
CHIPPING
GUMSTOOL HILL
CHISTOOL ST
LOVE LANE
DAVELS
DAMSEL
THE
GASTRELL
CROFT
BEECHTREE GDNS
HODGES CL
PARK RD
PRIORY GDNS
THE FOLLIES
NEW LEAZE GDNS
CONYGAR
WOODWARD CL
WISTARIA HILL
WHEATSHILL
ROMNEY RD
ELIZABETH LEAZE
CHESTNUT CL
OXLEAZE RD
WINDSOR RD
CORONATION
GROVE GDNS
UPTON GDNS
LONGTREE CL
ROAD BLIND
CHAVENAGE
HAMPTON STREET INDUSTRIAL ESTATE
PTON
BERKELEY
TALBOTS RD
HIGHFIELD RD
LOWFIELD GDNS
ST MARYS LANE
MAGDALEN COURT
St Marys C of E Junior School
CONYGAR
CONYGRE GDNS
ALEXANDER GDNS
MEAD
COTSWOLD CL
SHEPHERDS
RYLANDS
JACOBS CL
CHEVIOT
SUFFOLK CL
NORTHLAW
CLARIBE
BARTLEY
ROAD
LONDON ROAD
STREET
LONDON
Tetbury Sport & Leisure Centre
Sir William Romneys Community School
Highfield Farm
TETBURY INDUSTRIAL ESTATE
Supermarket
PRIORY INDUSTRIAL ESTATE
NORTHFIELD RD
SPRINGFIELDS
GLOUCESTER
NORTHLEAZE
CL
THE CIRENCESTER WAY
BRAMBROOK
NORTHFIELD CL
Tetbury

A   **B**   **C**   **D**

Gorse

WELSH WAY

Daglingworth Quarry
(Limestone)

Home
Farm

Bagendon Downs
Farm

WELSH

WAY

WELSH

WAY

LYNCROFT FARM
WORKSHOPS

Springfield
Farm

CUTHAM

A435

WELSH

CHELT

WARRENS GORSE GTS

Warrens Gorse
House

Forty Acre
Copse

Perrott's
Brook

MAYFIEL
MOBILE HOM

1

Peewits
House

Peewits
Hill

DOWERS LANE

DOWERS LA

ERMIN

Parso...
Copse

Smallbeech
Copse

Pewets
Copse

Trinity
Farm

CHELI
RO

2

ROMAN ROAD

South View
Farm

Cirencester
Golf Course

Club
House

3

Daglingworth
Place

Wellhill
Copse

WAY

Stratton
Park

Cemy

Grange
Farm

Playing
Field

LANE BAUNTON

LINKS VIEW

MANOR
CL

Clee
Hou

STRATTON
HEIGHTS

STRATTON
HEIGHTS

AISEY CT

GALLOWS POUND LA

CHUM
CT

4

5

SCHOOL HILL

GLOUCESTER

STREET

Daglingworth Stream

BAUNTON

POPES CT

TINGLESFIELD

THESSALY
RD

GRANGE

HARESFIELD

ELPHICK
RD

STRATTON

VALE
RD

GLEBE
CL

STRATTON

ROAD

PARK

WAY

HEIGHTS

QUARRY
CL

Stratton C of E
Primary School

Stratton

OVERHILL

ROAD

CLOSE

ROBERTS

ST JOHNS

CHELTENHAM

STRAT
MILL

Lo... eld

Stratton
Brook

Hotel

WAY

BARN

STRATTON
BROOK

DONSIDE

ROAD

STRATTON
PL

ALBION STREET

WHITEWAY

THE PYGHTELL

VW

A435

6

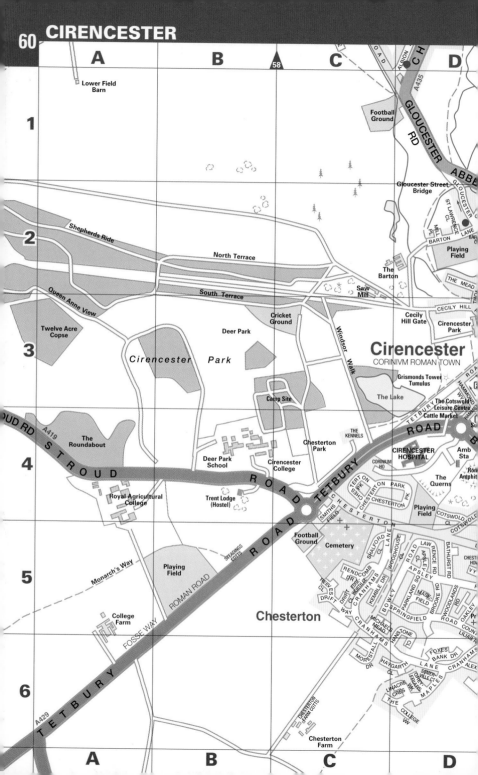

A **B** **C** **D**

1 — 6

Lower Field Barn

Football Ground

Gloucester Street Bridge

GLOUCESTER RD

ABBE

ALBION

A435

ST LAWRENCE CL

MILL PL

BARTON

LANE

GLOUCESTER LANE

Playing Field

THE MEAD

Shepherds Ride

North Terrace

South Terrace

Queen Anne View

The Barton

Saw Mill

Cecily Hill Gate

CECILY HILL

Cirencester Park

Twelve Acre Copse

Deer Park

Cricket Ground

Cirencester Park

Windsor Walk

Cirencester
CORINIVM ROMAN TOWN

Grismonds Tower Tumulus

The Lake

The Cotswold Leisure Centre

Cattle Market

HAMMOND

ROA

TETBURY

ROAD

Camp Site

Chesterton Park

THE KENNELS

CIRENCESTER HOSPITAL

CORINIVM HO

Amb Sta

Ron Amphit

OUD RD

A419

STROUD

The Roundabout

Deer Park School

Cirencester College

ROAD

TETBURY

CHESTERTON

CHESTERTON PARK

CHESTERTON

The Querns

Playing Field

COTSWOLD

COTSWOL

CHEST HO

VY

Royal Agricultural College

Trent Lodge (Hostel)

SMITHS FIELD

Football Ground

Cemetery

SHALFORD CL

WOODHOUSE

LAW.

APSLEY

APSLEY SQ

LAWRENCE RD

MASE FIELD

BATHURST RD

CHEST

Monarch's Way

Playing Field

ROMAN ROAD

STEADINGS COTTS

RENDCOMB DR

REEVES CL DRIFT

CRANHAMS

DRIFT EDGE

KEMBLE DR

MORLAND WAY

BOSWORTH

PARKLAND

SPRINGFIELD

BROOKE DR

WOODLANDS RD

OAKLEY

COUN

Pr

LILIAS

College Farm

FOSSE WAY

MICHAEL MEAD

STANSTONE RD

Chesterton

CRANHAMS

FOXES BANK DR

SPIRES CTES

LEWIS WK

MAPLE

THE COLLEGE

CRANHAMS

ALEX

A429

TETBURY

MORESTALL DR

HAYGARTH CL

LINACRE CRES

CHESTERTON FARM COTTS

Chesterton Farm

A **B** **C** **D**

A B4425 **B** AKEMAN STREE **C** Little Ackey **D**

ROMAN ROAD

B4425 STREET AKEMAN STREET

1

Crucis Park Farm Cotts

Crucis Park Farm

Unde

Merrillhill Farm

Norcote

Merrillhill Copse

Sou Ampne

Norcote Farm & Workshops

Merrill Hill

2

A417 LANE

Norcote House

Sidelands Copse

61 LONDON

A417

Ampney Par

3

Witpit Copse

LANE

Quarry House

R O A

WITPIT

4

Watert Stable

LANE

61

WITPIT LANE

5 **Preston**

Farm

MILDREDS FARM BARNS

VILLAGE FARM

St Augustine Farm

6

A419

A CI **B** **65** **C** **D**

ington use

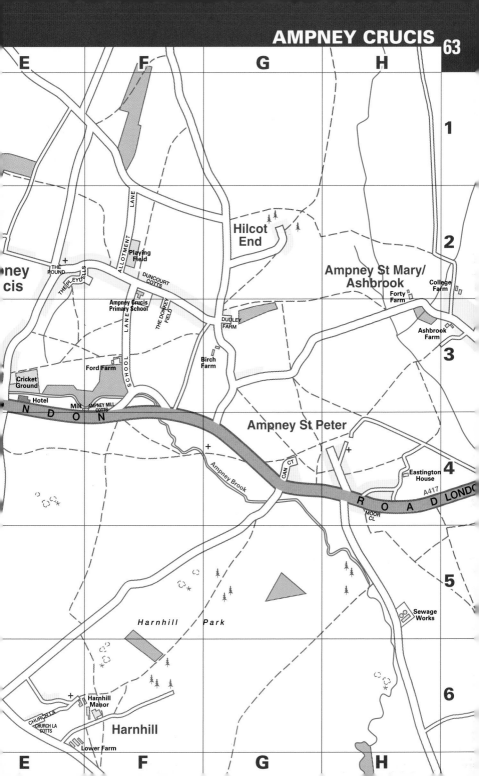

E   F   G   H

1

Hilcot
End

2

ney
cis

Ampney St Mary/
Ashbrook

THE
ROUND

College
Farm

THE PLEYD

Forty
Farm

ALLOTMENT LANE

Playing
Field

DUNCOURT
COTTS

Ampney Crucis
Primary School

Ashbrook
Farm

THE DONKEY FIELD

DUDLEY
FARM

3

LANE

SCHOOL

Ford Farm

Birch
Farm

Cricket
Ground

Hotel

Mill

AMPNEY MILL
COTTS

N D O N

Ampney St Peter

CAN CT

Ampney Brook

4

Eastington
House

A417

R O A D LONDO

MOOR
CL

5

Harnhill   Park

Sewage
Works

CHURCH LA

CHURCH LA
COTTS

Harnhill
Manor

6

Harnhill

Lower Farm

E   F   G   H

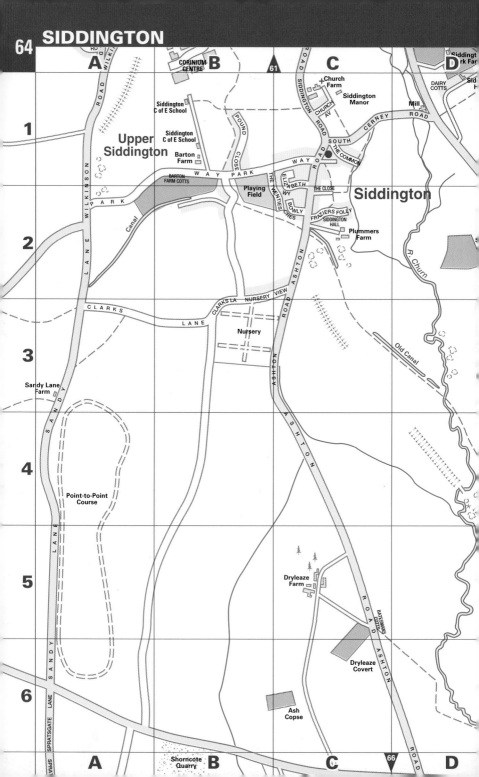

A · B · C · D

Upper Siddington

Siddington

CORINIUM CENTRE

Siddington C of E School

Siddington C of E School

Church Farm

Siddington Manor

Mill

DAIRY COTTS

Barton Farm

BARTON FARM COTTS

Playing Field

THE CLOSE

FRAZIERS FOLLY

SIDDINGTON HALL

Plummers Farm

Canal

R. Churn

CLARKS LANE

CLARKS LA

NURSERY VIEW

Old Canal

Nursery

Sandy Lane Farm

Point-to-Point Course

Dryleaze Farm

BATESMANS COTTS

Dryleaze Covert

Ash Copse

Shorncote Quarry

SPRATSGATE LANE

E   F   62   G   H

IRENCESTER

ERMIN WAY ROMAN ROAD

Playing
Field

Ermin
Farm

GRAY
RD

CRES

THOMPSON
RD

HANNAH
ROAD

JACKSON
RD

AARON
RD

MOTTERS-
HEAD RD

SOUTH CERNEY
ARMY STATION

TRENCHARD GDNS

TRENCHARD GDN

TRENCHARD

AMPLEDON

GARDENS

ROAD

A417

A419

A419

CIRENCESTER ROAD

CIRENCESTER RD

CIRENCESTER ROAD

Airfield

Sewage
Works

The Butts
Farm

L A N E

Quarry
Farm

N O R T H M O O R

Dismantled Railway

Hill View
Farm

Castle
(site of)

SILVER

STREET

EDWARDS
COLLEGE

W O W

Chapter
Manor

TIMBRELLS
CL

CHURCH LA

BOW WOW

SCHOOL LA
CL

River Ch

MILL

OXBUSH

BOXBRUSH
RD

BOW WOW

THE
CLOSE

ROBERT FRAN

ROBERT

LANE

66

E   F   G   H

1

2

3

4

5

6

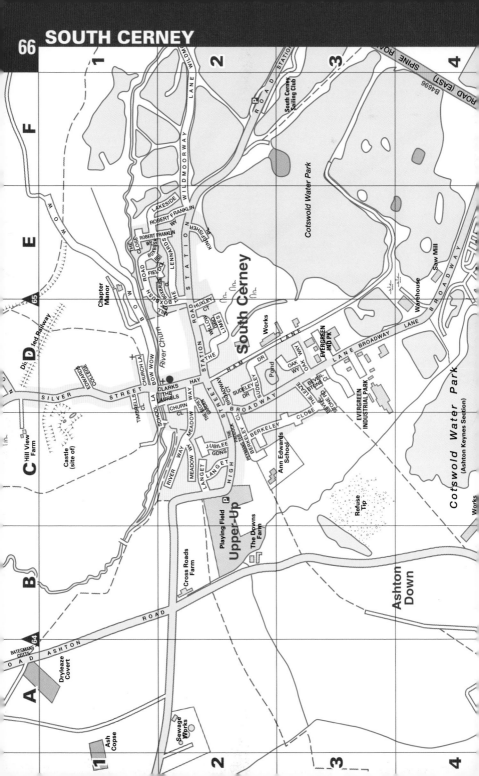

South Cerney

Cotswold Water Park

South Cerney Sailing Club

Cotswold Water Park
(Ashton Keynes Section)

Ashton Down

Upper Up

Playing Field

The Downs Farm

Cross Roads Farm

Refuse Tip

Chapter Manor

Castle (site of)

Hill View Farm

Batesmans Cotts

Dryleaze Covert

Ash Copse

Sewage Works

Works

Warehouse

Saw Mill

EVERGREEN IND PK

EVERGREEN INDUSTRIAL PARK

Ann Edwards School

Edwards College

River Churn

Chapter Manor

LAKESIDE
ROBERT FRANKLIN
ROBERT FRANKLIN WY
THE CLOSE
BOTBUSH
FIELD
KNIGHTSFISHER
WILDMOORWAY LANE
STATION ROAD
THE LENNARDS
HUXLEY CT
WILLOW GRO
THE LIMES
HAM STREET
STATION ROAD
THE STREET
SUDELEY DR
SUDELEY DR
OAK WAY
OAK WY
LANE
POND
BROADWAY
BROADWAY
BROADWAY LANE
THE CLEEZE
BEVER STONE CL
CLOSE
BERKELEY
BERKELEY
PENNSLEY DR
PADDOCK CLOSE
BROADWAY
THE ROOKERY
MEADOW WY
HAY
SCHOOL LA
CHURN CL
CHURCH LA
BOW WOW
TIMBRELLS LA
SILVER STREET
SILVER STREET
HIGH STREET
RIVER WAY
MEADOW VW
LANGET
LANGET
JUBILEE GDNS
CLARKS
THE LAURELS
SPINE ROAD (EAST) B4696
ROAD (EAST) B4696
STATION ROAD
Dis[used] Railway

ROAD
ASHTON ROAD
SILVER STREET

Ashton Keynes

North End

Derry Fields

Wheatleys Barn Farm

Works

Rixon Farm

Guest Farm

Westfields Farm

Sports Ground

Kentend Farm

Clayhill Copse

Ring & Bailey

North End Farm

Furze Brake

Freeth's Wood

Playing Field

Playing Field

Ashton Keynes Primary School

Derryfields Farm

Thames Path

Thames Path

FRIDAYS HAM LANE

FRIDAYS HAM LANE

OXON GATE

WEST SPINE ROAD

WHITEFRIARS

LEAZE

SPINE ROAD

COXS

IND EST

HILL BACK

CHURCH HW

CHURCH WK

HIGH ROAD

THE LEAZE

STREET

KENET END

RICHMOND CT

COWE HO GDNS

FORE STREET

KENT END

ASHFIELD

HARRISD

MILLING

SKINNERS CL

PARK PL

EASTGE

PARK PARK

ASTHELD

THE LOTTS

FOUR ACRE CL

THE MEAD

HAPPY LAND

PL THAMES

BIRCH

GLADE

HIGH ROAD

DERRY ROAD

HIGH ROAD

GOSDITCH

DAIRY FARM

THE

B4696

R. Thames or Isis

HIGH ROAD HIGH ROAD

Ash Plantation

Slate Purlieu

Blackbird Cottage

Park Leaze Barn

Canal (disused)

New Covert

TRIANGLE COTTS

Ewen Manor

Thames Path

Home Farm

Ewen

THE TIMBRELLS

Brooklands Farm

A429

Severall's Copse

Dismantled Railway

Mill Farm

River Thames or Isis

Parkers Bridge

Park Covert

Clayfurlong Farm

Kemble

SCHOOL ROAD

CHURCH ROAD

KEMBLE PK

Kemble House

The Vicarage

Kemble County Primary School

Hall

THAMES DR

WEST LANE

LIMES ROAD

Home Farm

Playing Field

WINDMILL

CLAY FURLONG LA

OAK LA

ORCHARD GRO

GLEBE LA

WINDMILL COTTS

STATION ROAD

WEST HAY GRO

RAIL-WAY TER

WEST ROAD

VICARAGE LA

OLD

THE OAKS

Kemble Tunnel

KEMBLE

Field Barn

Highstubs Plantation

A429

FOSSE WY (Roman Rd)

A433

dex includes some
for which there is
cient space on the
These names are
ed by an * and are
ed by the nearest
ng thoroughfare.

Bedford St, Stroud GL5 — 6 C3
Beech Cl, Cheltenham GL52 — 13 G2
Beech Cl, Highnam GL2 — 7 B2
Beech Cl, Quedgeley GL2 — 28 A6
Beech Gro, Cirencester GL7 — 61 F3
Beech Gro, Stroud GL5 — 44 B4
Beech La GL6 — 46 B4
Beech Tree Gdns GL8 — 57 D2
Beechcroft Rd GL2 — 21 F4
Beeches Cl GL10 — 42 D2
Beeches Grn GL5 — 6 B2
Beeches Rd, Cheltenham GL53 — 17 F4
Beeches Rd, Cirencester GL7 — 61 F3
Beechmore Dr GL51 — 15 F6
Beechurst Av GL52 — 12 D5
Beechurst Wy GL52 — 13 F6
Beechwood Cl GL52 — 13 F6
Beechwood Dr GL6 — 46 B3
Beechwood Gro, Gloucester GL4 — 29 G2
Beechwood Gro, Wotton-under-Edge GL12 — 56 F2
Beechwood Shopping Centre GL52 — 5 D4
Belfry Cl GL4 — 26 A3
Belgrave Rd GL1 — 4 E4
Belgrove Ter GL1 — 25 E4
Bell La, Gloucester GL1 — 4 D3
Bell La, Minchinhampton GL6 — 49 G2
Bell La, Selsley GL5 — 43 H2
Bell Walk GL1 — 4 C3
Bella Vista GL52 — 9 E3
Belland Dr GL53 — 17 E4
Belle Vue Cl GL5 — 6 D2
Belle Vue Rd GL5 — 6 D3
Belmont Av GL3 — 26 D5
Belmont Rd, Cheltenham GL52 — 5 D2
Belmont Rd, Stroud GL5 — 41 F6
Belmore Pl GL53 — 5 C6
Belvedere Mews GL6 — 46 C5
Belworth Cl GL51 — 15 G4
Belworth Dr GL51 — 15 G4
Benhall Av GL51 — 15 E3
Benhall Gdns GL51 — 15 E3
Bennington St GL50 — 5 C3
Benson Cl GL4 — 26 B5
Berkeley Cl, Cirencester GL7 — 66 C2
Berkeley Cl, Stroud GL5 — 39 G5
Berkeley Ct GL2 — 5 D4
Berkeley Pl GL52 — 5 D5
Berkeley Rd GL7 — 61 E6
Berkeley St, Cheltenham GL52 — 5 D5
Berkeley St, Gloucester GL1 — 4 C2
Berkeley Wy GL8 — 57 C1
Berrells Rd GL8 — 57 C4
Berry Cl GL6 — 35 F2
Berry Hill Cres GL7 — 61 E1
Berry Hill Rd GL7 — 61 E1
Berry Lawn GL4 — 30 D3
Berryfield GL5 — 44 A4
Berryfield Glade GL3 — 22 D3
Berrymore Rd GL5 — 44 A4
Berwick Rd GL52 — 8 D1
Besbury La GL6 — 49 F1
Besbury Pk GL6 — 49 H1
Bethesda St GL50 — 16 B1
Betjeman Cl GL2 — 29 E1
Bettridge Ct GL52 — 13 F3
Betworthy Est GL11 — 53 H6
Beverley Cft GL51 — 14 D1
Beverley Gdns GL52 — 9 F2
Beverstone Cl GL7 — 66 D3
Beverstone Rd GL7 — 66 D3
Bewley Wy GL3 — 22 D3
Beyon Cl GL11 — 54 B1
Beyon Dr GL11 — 54 B1
Bibury Rd, Cheltenham GL51 — 15 E3
Bibury Rd, Gloucester GL4 — 25 E5
Bicks La GL54 — 7 C5
Bijou Ct GL1 — 21 E6
Bilberry Cl GL4 — 31 F1
Billbrook Rd GL3 — 26 D4
Billingham Cl GL4 — 25 G5

Billings Wy GL50 — 15 H5
Bingham Cl GL7 — 61 E3
Binyon Rd GL54 — 7 A6
Birch Av GL4 — 25 G5
Birch Cl, Charlton Kings GL53 — 17 G4
Birch Cl, Cheltenham GL52 — 9 E2
Birch Glade SN6 — 67 C8
Birch Rd, Dursley GL11 — 54 D3
Birch Rd, Stroud GL5 — 44 B3
Birchall Av GL4 — 30 C3
Birchall La GL4 — 30 D3
Birches Cl GL5 — 6 D2
Birches Dr GL5 — 6 C2
Birchfield Rd GL52 — 9 E2
Birchley Rd GL52 — 13 E6
Birchmore Rd GL1 — 25 F3
Birchwood Flds GL4 — 29 G2
Bird Rd GL3 — 26 D6
Birds Crossing GL5 — 44 B5
Birdwood Cl GL4 — 31 E1
Birkeley Cl GL3 — 27 E5
Bishop Rd GL51 — 18 C3
Bishops Castle Wy GL1 — 25 F4
Bishops Cl, Cheltenham GL52 — 8 D3
Bishops Cl, Stroud GL5 — 40 D6
Bishops Cleeve By-Pass GL52 — 8 B2
Bishops Dr GL52 — 8 C3
Bishops Mdw GL52 — 8 C2
Bishops Rd GL4 — 26 B5
Bishops Walk GL7 — 61 E3
Bishopstone Cl GL51 — 14 D2
Bishopstone Rd GL1 — 25 F3
Bisley Old Rd GL5 — 41 E5
Bisley Rd, Cheltenham GL51 — 15 F3
Bisley Rd, Gloucester GL4 — 29 G4
Bisley Rd, Oakridge GL6 — 47 G1
Bisley Rd, Stroud GL5 — 41 E6
Bisley St GL6 — 35 G2
Bittern Av GL4 — 25 H5
Blaby Cl GL4 — 26 C6
Black Bird Ct GL9 — 38 D4
Black Dog Wy GL1 — 4 D1
Black Horse Hill GL8 — 57 C3
Black Jack St GL7 — 61 E3
Blackberry Cl GL4 — 31 E1
Blackberry Fld GL52 — 13 G3
Blackberry Gro GL52 — 8 C2
Blackbird Av GL3 — 22 A3
Blackboys GL11 — 55 C5
Blackburn Rd GL52 — 8 C5
Blackfriars GL1 — 4 C3
Blacklow Cl GL5 — 44 A4
Blackquarries Hill GL12 — 56 F2
Blacksmith La, Cheltenham GL52 — 13 F2
Blacksmith La, Gloucester GL3 — 23 F5
Blacksmiths Grnd GL2 — 7 B1
Blackthorn End GL53 — 15 H6
Blackthorn Gdns GL2 — 28 B4
Blackwater Wy GL2 — 22 A4
Blackwells GL11 — 55 E8
Bladon Mews GL51 — 14 C3
Blaisdon Cl GL4 — 31 E1
Blaisdon Wy GL51 — 11 E4
Blake Cft GL51 — 11 E5
Blake Hill Wy GL4 — 26 A5
Blake Rd GL7 — 61 E2
Blakeley Ct*, Cheltenham Rd East GL3 — 22 C3
Blakeney Cl GL4 — 29 F2
Blakewell Mead GL5 — 35 F2
Bleasby Gdns GL51 — 15 H3
Blenheim Cl GL54 — 7 B5
Blenheim Orch GL51 — 18 C3
Blenheim Rd GL1 — 25 E3
Blenheim Sq GL51 — 11 F6
Blind La GL51 — 57 C1
Blinkhorns Bridge La GL2 — 25 G2
Bloombury St GL51 — 12 A4
Bloomfield Rd GL1 — 24 C5
Bloomfield Ter GL1 — 24 C5
Blue Boys Pk GL6 — 49 G2
Blue Quarry Rd GL7 — 61 G3
Bluebell Chase GL6 — 46 C2
Bluebell Dr GL7 — 61 G6
Bluebell Gro GL51 — 15 G6
Bluebell Rise GL6 — 46 C2
Boakes Dr GL10 — 38 B5

Bodenham Fld GL4 — 26 A5
Bodiam Av GL4 — 28 D3
Bodman Rd GL51 — 11 F5
Boleyn Cl GL3 — 22 C2
Bondend Rd GL4 — 31 F3
Bootenhay Rd GL52 — 9 E1
Borage Cl GL4 — 26 C6
Borough Cl GL10 — 42 D3
Boscombe La GL6 — 51 A2
Bospin La GL5 — 44 A5
Boulton La GL11 — 55 E7
Boulton Rd GL50 — 12 B2
Bouncers La GL52 — 13 F4
Bourne La GL5 — 45 G4
Bournside Cl GL51 — 15 H4
Bournside Ct GL51 — 15 H4
Bournside Dr GL51 — 15 H4
Bournside Rd GL51 — 15 H4
Bourton Rd GL4 — 29 G3
Boverton Av GL3 — 32 B2
Boverton Dr GL3 — 32 A1
Bow Wow GL7 — 66 D1
Bowbridge La, Cheltenham GL52 — 13 F2
Bowbridge La, Stroud GL5 — 41 E6
Bowbridge Lock GL5 — 45 E1
Bowen Cl GL52 — 13 E3
Bowers Lea GL11 — 54 B2
Bowl Hill GL5 — 44 B3
Bowling Green Av GL7 — 61 E1
Bowling Green La GL1 — 60 D1
Bowling Green Rd GL7 — 60 D1
Bowly Cres GL7 — 64 C2
Bowly Rd, Cirencester GL7 — 60 C5
Bowly Rd, Gloucester GL1 — 24 C6
Bownham Mead GL5 — 44 D4
Bownham Pk GL5 — 44 D5
Box Cres GL6 — 49 F2
Box Gdns*, Box Cres GL6 — 49 F2
Box La GL6 — 49 E3
Box Rd GL11 — 52 D6
Box Road Av GL11 — 52 D5
Boxbrush Cl GL7 — 66 E2
Boxbrush Rd GL7 — 66 D2
Boyce Cl GL4 — 31 E2
Bracelands GL6 — 46 C1
Bradford Rd GL2 — 25 G1
Bradley Cl GL2 — 21 H5
Bradley Rd, Cheltenham GL53 — 17 E4
Bradley Rd, Wotton-under-Edge GL12 — 56 B1
Bradley St GL12 — 56 C2
Bradshaw Cl GL2 — 22 A4
Brae Walk GL4 — 30 D1
Braeburn Cl, Cheltenham GL51 — 11 F6
Braeburn Cl, Gloucester GL2 — 25 H1
Bramble Chase GL52 — 8 C2
Bramble Dr GL11 — 54 C4
Bramble La GL10 — 38 D4
Bramble Lawn GL4 — 30 D3
Bramble Rise GL52 — 13 G3
Bramley Mews GL4 — 26 C5
Bramley Rd GL51 — 11 F6
Branch Hill Rise GL53 — 17 E4
Branch Rd GL51 — 14 B4
Brandon Cl GL3 — 22 C1
Brandon Pl GL50 — 16 B2
Brantwood Rd GL6 — 47 E3
Braybrooke Gdns GL8 — 57 D2
Brecon Cl GL2 — 28 A5
Bregawn Cl GL52 — 8 C4
Breinton Wy GL2 — 22 A5
Brensham Ct GL3 — 26 D4
Brevel Ter GL53 — 17 F3
Brewery La, Brimscombe GL5 — 45 F4
Brewery La, Nailsworth GL6 — 48 B5
Brewery Yd GL5 — 39 H5
Briar Cl GL3 — 41 E3
Briar Lawn GL4 — 30 D3
Briar Walk GL4 — 30 D3
Briarbank Rise GL52 — 17 G2
Briars Cl GL3 — 22 C3
Brick Row GL5 — 6 D3
Brickfields GL12 — 56 D4
Bridge Cl, Cirencester GL7 — 61 F5

Bridge Cl, Gloucester GL2 — 24 A5
Bridge End GL7 — 61 E5
Bridge Fm GL2 — 20 A2
Bridge Mead GL5 — 39 G6
Bridge Rd, Cirencester GL7 — 61 F5
Bridge Rd, Gloucester GL2 — 36 A3
Bridge Rd, Stroud GL5 — 39 G6
Bridge St, Cheltenham GL51 — 11 H5
Bridge St, Nailsworth GL6 — 48 C4
Bridge St, Stroud GL5 — 40 A6
Bridgend Cl GL10 — 38 C6
Bridgend Rd GL51 — 14 D4
Bridgeside GL5 — 40 A6
Brierley Cl GL4 — 26 B6
Brighouse Cl GL4 — 26 B2
Brighton Rd GL52 — 12 D5
Brimley GL10 — 42 D2
Brimscombe Hill GL5 — 45 G5
Brimscombe La GL5 — 45 G5
Brimsome Mdw GL2 — 7 B1
Brindle Cl GL4 — 30 C1
Brionne Wy GL2 — 21 G4
Brisbane GL10 — 38 C3
Bristol Rd, Cirencester GL7 — 60 D4
Bristol Rd, Gloucester GL2 — 33 B3
Bristol Rd, Stonehouse GL10 — 38 A5
Bristol Rd, Stroud GL2 — 52 C3
Britannia Wy GL52 — 9 E2
Brizen La GL53 — 18 F1
Broad Leys Rd GL4 — 26 A4
Broad Oak Wy GL51 — 15 F5
Broad St GL10 — 42 D3
Broadfield Rd GL10 — 37 A5
Broadmere GL11 — 54 B4
Broadmere Cl GL11 — 54 A4
Broadstone Cl GL4 — 26 B3
Broadway GL4 — 25 E6
Broadway Cl GL52 — 13 E2
Broadway Ct GL52 — 66 D2
Broadway La GL7 — 66 D2
Broadwell GL11 — 55 E6
Broadwell Cl GL4 — 26 B6
Broadwell Ter GL11 — 55 E6
Brock Cl GL51 — 14 C5
Brockeridge Cl GL2 — 28 A3
Brockley Acres GL6 — 46 C1
Brockley Rd GL10 — 42 C2
Brockworth GL3 — 32 A2
Brockworth By-Pass GL3 — 32 C1
Brockworth Rd GL2 — 26 C6
Brome Rd GL4 — 26 C6
Bronte Cl GL51 — 15 F4
Brook Cl GL54 — 7 A6
Brook Ct GL50 — 16 A3
Brook Rd GL51 — 11 H5
Brook St GL1 — 25 E4
Brook Vale GL52 — 17 E1
Brookbank Cl GL51 — 12 A4
Brooke Rd GL7 — 60 D5
Brookfield La GL3 — 23 G4
Brookfield Rd, Churchdown GL3 — 23 F5
Brookfield Rd, Hucclecote GL3 — 26 B4
Brooklands Pk GL3 — 21 H4
Brooklyn Cl GL51 — 11 G5
Brooklyn Ct GL51 — 11 G5
Brooklyn Gdns GL51 — 11 G5
Brooklyn Rd GL51 — 15 F1
Brooksdale La GL53 — 16 B2
Brookside Villas GL2 — 25 G1
Brookthorpe Cl GL4 — 29 F2
Brookway Dr GL53 — 17 E3
Brookway Rd GL53 — 17 E2
Brosnan Dr GL51 — 14 D2
Brown Cl GL51 — 11 E5
Brownings La GL11 — 55 E6
Browns La GL10 — 38 D6
Browns Piece GL12 — 56 D3
Brownshill GL6 — 46 A4
Brownshill Rd GL6 — 46 A4
Brunel Cl GL2 — 33 F1
Brunel Wy GL10 — 38 A4
Brunswest GL1 — 4 C4
Brunswick St GL1 — 4 C4
Brunswick Rd GL1 — 4 C4
Brunswick Sq GL1 — 4 C4
Brunswick St GL50 — 5 B2

Bruton Wy GL1
Bryaston Cl GL51
Bryerland Rd GL3
Brymore Av GL52
Brymore Cl GL52
Buckholt Wy GL3
Buckingham Av GL51
Buckingham Cl GL10
Buckingham Dr GL51
Buckland Cl GL7
Buckles Cl GL53
Budding Rd GL10
Buddleia Cl GL4
Bull La, Cheltenham GL54
Bull La, Gloucester GL1
Bull Pitch GL11
Bullfinch Rd GL4
Bullfinch Wy GL3
Bullingham Ct GL51
Bunting Hill GL6
Bunting Wy GL6
Burcombe Rd GL4
Burcombe Wy GL6
Burdett Cl GL10
Burdett Rd GL10
Burford Av GL51
Burford Dr GL5
Burford Mews GL1
Burford Rd GL7
Burfords Grnd GL4
Burleigh Cft GL3
Burleigh La GL5
Burleigh Tor GL5
Burleigh Vw GL6
Burma Av GL52
Burma Rd GL6
Burnet Cl GL4
Burns Av GL2
Burnt Oak GL11
Burton St GL50
Bush Cl GL10
Bush Ct GL52
Bush Hay GL3
Bushcombe Cl GL52
Bushcombe Gdns GL3
Bushcombe La GL52
Bushy Wy GL51
Bussage Hill GL5
Butlers Cotts GL51
Butt Grn GL6
Butt St GL6
Buttercross La GL52
Buttercup Lawn GL4
Buttermere Cl GL51
Buttermilk La GL3
Butterow Hill GL5
Butterow La GL5
Butterow West GL5
Buttington Cl GL4
Button Mill Ind Est GL10
Butts Hill GL6
Butts La GL52
Butts Walk GL51
Byard Rd GL2
Bybrook Gdns GL4
Bybrook Rd GL4
Byfield Cl GL52
Byron Av GL2
Byron Bank GL53
Byron Rd, Cheltenham GL51
Byron Rd, Dursley GL11
Byron Rd, Stroud GL5

Cadbury Cl GL3
Caernarvon Cl GL51
Caernarvon Cl GL51
Caernarvon Rd GL51
Caesar Rd GL2
Caine Sq GL11
Cainscross Rd GL5
Cakebridge Pl GL52
Cakebridge Rd GL52
Calderdale GL4
Calderwood Ct GL50
Caledonian Rd GL4
Calspick Wy GL2
Calton Rd GL1
Calverley Mews GL51
Cam Grn GL11
Cam Pitch GL11
Cam Rd GL52
Camberley Cl GL51
Camberwell Rd GL51
Cambray Ct, Cheltenham GL50

y Ct,
ester GL7 61 E3
y Pl GL50 5 C5
dge Av,
nham GL51 15 G1
dge Av,
y GL11 55 E8
dge St GL1 4 E4
dge Wy GL6 49 F2
Walk GL2 28 B4
Ct GL51 15 G6
ile Cl GL4 26 C6
d GL52 13 F6
ell Cl GL3 22 B2
en Rd,
nham GL51 15 E2
en Rd,
ester GL4 29 G3
n Cl GL4 30 A1
n Pk GL51 18 E1
GL7 63 G4
onworks
GL5 45 F4
y GL2 20 A5
a GL10 38 C3
Rd GL2 22 A5
Court Mews
56 A1
ury Walk GL51 15 G5
Acre GL6 35 G1
Ct GL52 8 C4
Dr GL52 8 C4
t,
nham GL52 13 F2
t, Stroud GL5 40 D4
d GL4 30 C3
Pk GL2 29 E1
Barton Cl GL5 41 F4
Dr GL2 28 D4
oke Dr GL52 17 G2
Gdns GL5 6 C4
Pl GL50 5 A1
St GL52 12 D6
Gro GL51 11 E5
then Rd GL51 15 E5
then St GL1 25 E4
l GL4 25 H2
ers La GL7 61 E3
ooke Rd GL3 26 D5
ro GL51 11 E5
t GL2 33 D1
d GL51 11 G4
Orch GL2 28 C4
Wy GL6 48 A3
line Fld GL4 26 B5
l GL1 25 F2
Green Rd GL5 39 G4
l GL6 35 F2
otts GL4 26 B3
t GL5 6 D4
ill Dr GL3 32 C3
Mead GL10 42 D3
Meads Wy GL1 4 A3
Mews GL7 60 D3
itch GL5 6 D5
ise GL5 6 D5
ow GL10 42 D3
t,
nham GL54 7 C6
t,
ester GL7 60 D3
t, Dursley GL11 55 D6
t,
house GL10 42 D3
t, Stroud GL5 6 D4
tream Ct*,
ll Mews GL11 55 F7
elds Av GL52 17 G3
elds Dr GL52 17 G3
elds Rd GL52 17 G3
aine Dr GL51 14 D2
ead Rd GL5 6 A6
eads Ct GL1 4 A2
n Rd GL4 26 A4
Ct GL11 55 F7
Mews GL11 55 F7
be Cl GL52 8 B2
al Ct GL1 25 F1
nes Cl GL5 41 F5
l GL2 28 B6
od Ct GL5 41 F3
ish Av GL3 23 F4
GL6 49 G2
GL1 24 C5
ill GL7 60 D3
l,
nham GL53 17 F4

Cedar Cl, Stroud GL5 39 G6
Cedar Court Rd GL53 5 C6
Cedar Dr GL11 55 D6
Cedar Gdns GL10 38 D4
Cedar Gro GL54 7 B5
Cedar Rd GL3 32 A1
Cedarwood Dr GL4 29 G2
Celandine Bank GL52 9 E2
Cellars Rd GL2 28 A6
Cemetery Rd GL4 25 F5
Central Cross Dr GL52 12 C3
Central Rd, Gloucester GL1 24 D4
Central Rd, Stroud GL5 40 A5
Central Wy GL51 11 H6
Centurion Cl GL4 26 B5
Century Cl GL7 61 G2
Century Ct GL50 16 B1
Cetenary Mews*, Cheltenham Rd East GL3 22 C3
Chaceley Cl, Abbeymead GL4 26 B6
Chaceley Cl, Quadgeley GL2 28 A5
Chad Rd GL51 15 G2
Chadbournes GL3 23 E3
Chadwick Cl GL4 29 F3
Chaffinch Cl GL3 21 H2
Chaffinch Ct GL10 38 C4
Chalford Av GL51 14 C4
Chalford Ind Est GL6 46 C5
Chalford Rd GL4 29 G4
Chamwells Av GL2 21 G5
Chamwells Walk GL2 21 G5
Chancel Cl GL4 25 G3
Chancel Pk GL53 17 E2
Chancel Wy GL53 17 E2
Chandler Rd GL52 8 C4
Chandos Ct GL54 7 B5
Chandos Dr GL3 32 C3
Chandos Rd GL5 44 B1
Chandos St GL54 7 B5
Chantry Ct GL8 57 D3
Chantry Gate GL52 8 C4
Chapel Gdns GL2 33 D1
Chapel Hay Cl GL3 23 F5
Chapel Hay La GL3 23 F5
Chapel Hill, Amberley GL5 48 C1
Chapel Hill, Oakridge GL6 47 H2
Chapel La, Cheltenham GL52 9 F3
Chapel La, Ebley GL5 39 G5
Chapel La, Minchinhampton GL6 49 G3
Chapel Row GL10 38 C5
Chapel St, Cheltenham GL50 5 A3
Chapel St, Dursley GL11 54 C2
Chapel St, Stroud GL5 6 D4
Chapel Walk GL50 5 B4
Chapman Wy GL51 15 G4
Chargrove Bsns Centre GL51 18 D1
Chargrove La GL51 15 E6
Charlecote Av GL4 29 E5
Charlecote Cnr GL52 8 C3
Charles St, Cheltenham GL51 12 A4
Charles St, Gloucester GL1 4 F4
Charlies Wy GL3 27 E4
Charlock Cl GL4 30 A1
Charlton Cl GL53 17 E4
Charlton Court Rd GL52 17 E2
Charlton Ct GL1 4 F2
Charlton Dr GL53 16 D2
Charlton Kings Ind Est GL53 17 E5
Charlton La GL53 16 B4
Charlton La Centre GL53 16 C4
Charlton Park Dr GL53 16 D2
Charlton Park Gate GL53 16 D3
Charlton Rd GL8 57 B3
Charlton Wy GL2 21 H4
Charnwood Cl GL53 16 B4
Charnwood Rd GL53 16 B4
Chase Av GL52 17 G3
Chase La GL4 25 G4
Chasely Cres GL51 15 F6
Chasewood Cnr GL6 46 B3
Chatcombe Cl GL53 17 F4
Chatcombe Rd GL4 30 B1
Chatsworth Av GL1 29 E4

Chatsworth Dr GL53 16 C5
Chaucer Cl GL1 24 C6
Chavenage La GL8 57 A1
Cheapside GL5 6 B4
Chedworth Rd GL4 29 G2
Chedworth Wy GL51 15 E3
Chelbury Mews GL52 13 E3
Chelmsford Av GL51 15 H6
Chelsea Cl GL53 16 D1
Chelsea Ct GL1 4 C3
Chelt Rd GL52 13 F4
Cheltenham & Gloucester Nuffield Hospital GL51 14 C3
Cheltenham General Hospital GL53 16 C1
Cheltenham Ind Pk GL51 11 H6
Cheltenham Rd, Bishops Cleeve GL52 8 C6
Cheltenham Rd, Cirencester GL7 58 D1
Cheltenham Rd, Gloucester GL2 21 G6
Cheltenham Rd, Stroud GL6 35 G2
Cheltenham Rd, Winchcombe GL54 7 A6
Cheltenham Rd East GL3 22 B4
Chequers Rd GL4 25 F4
Cheriton Cl GL51 15 F6
Cherrington Dr GL4 26 B6
Cherry Av GL53 17 G4
Cherry Blossom Cl GL52 8 C1
Cherry Cl GL2 28 A6
Cherry Ct GL52 13 F6
Cherry Gdns GL3 26 C3
Cherry Orch GL12 56 E3
Cherry Orchard Rd GL8 57 D2
Cherry Tree Cl GL6 48 A4
Cherry Tree Dr GL7 61 G5
Cherrytree La GL7 61 H1
Cherrywood Gdns GL4 29 G2
Cherston Ct GL4 26 B3
Chervil Cl GL4 30 B1
Cheshire Rd GL3 22 B3
Chesmann Ct GL1 21 E5
Chestal GL11 55 E6
Chester Cres GL7 61 E4
Chester Mews GL7 61 F4
Chester Rd GL4 25 H3
Chester St GL7 61 E3
Chester Walk GL50 5 B3
Chesterton Farm Cotts GL7 60 C6
Chesterton Gro GL7 61 E5
Chesterton Ho GL7 60 D5
Chesterton La GL7 60 C4
Chesterton Link GL7 61 E5
Chesterton Pk GL7 60 C4
Chestnut Av GL10 38 C4
Chestnut Cl, Abbeymead GL2 26 B6
Chestnut Cl, Quedgeley GL2 28 B6
Chestnut Cl, Stroud GL6 48 B5
Chestnut Cl, Tetbury GL8 57 B2
Chestnut Cotts GL2 7 B1
Chestnut Hill GL6 48 B5
Chestnut La GL5 40 A5
Chestnut Pl GL53 18 F1
Chestnut Ter GL53 17 E3
Chestnut Walk GL53 17 E3
Cheviot Cl, Gloucester GL2 28 B6
Cheviot Cl, Tetbury GL8 57 D1
Cheviot Rd GL52 13 F3
Cheyney Cl GL4 25 G5
Chillingworth Mews GL1 4 C4
Chiltern Av GL52 8 B2
Chiltern Rd, Cheltenham GL52 13 F3
Chiltern Rd, Gloucester GL2 28 A5
Chipping Cl GL12 56 C3
Chipping Gdns GL12 56 C3
Chipping St GL8 57 D3
Chipping Steps GL8 57 D3
Chislet Wy GL4 29 F4
Chivenor Wy GL2 28 D4
Choirs Cl GL4 26 B5
Chosen Dr GL3 22 D5
Chosen View Rd GL51 11 H4
Chosen Wy GL3 26 C3
Christchurch Rd GL50 15 H3
Christowe La GL53 16 C2
Chum Ct GL7 58 D5

Church Av GL7 64 C1
Church Cotts GL52 13 G2
Church Dr GL2 28 B5
Church End GL6 49 E2
Church La, Ampney Crucis GL7 63 E6
Church La, Barnwood GL4 26 A3
Church La, Gloucester GL2 36 B1
Church La, Prestbury GL52 13 F2
Church La, Shurdington GL51 18 C3
Church La, South Cerney GL7 66 D1
Church La, Stonehouse GL10 38 B6
Church La, Stroud GL5 48 C1
Church La, Swindon SN6 67 C7
Church La, Tuffley GL4 29 G5
Church La, Hardwicke GL2 33 A2
Church Lane Cotts GL7 63 E6
Church Piece GL53 17 F3
Church Pl GL5 44 B1
Church Rd, Bishops Cleeve GL52 8 C2
Church Rd, Cirencester GL7 68 B4
Church Rd, Dursley GL11 54 D4
Church Rd, Gloucester GL3 23 F5
Church Rd, Leckhampton GL53 16 B5
Church Rd, Longlevens GL2 21 H5
Church Rd, Maisemore GL2 20 A1
Church Rd, Stonehouse GL10 42 B3
Church Rd, Stroud GL5 39 H6
Church Rd, Swindon GL51 11 H2
Church Rd, Warden Hill GL51 15 G3
Church Rd, Windsoredge GL6 48 A3
Church Rd, Woodchester GL5 44 A4
Church Rise GL2 20 A2
Church St, Charlton Kings GL53 17 E3
Church St, Cheltenham GL50 5 B3
Church St, Cirencester GL7 61 F4
Church St, Gloucester GL2 4 B4
Church St, Nailsworth GL6 48 C5
Church St, Stonehouse GL10 42 D2
Church St, Stroud GL5 6 C3
Church St, Tetbury GL8 57 C3
Church St, Wotton-under-Edge GL12 56 D3
Church Vw GL51 10 D2
Church Walk, Cheltenham GL53 17 F3
Church Walk, Gloucester GL2 36 A6
Church Walk, Swindon SN6 67 C7
Church Walk, Wotton-under-Edge GL12 56 D3
Church Wy GL4 25 H5
Churchdown La GL3 26 D4
Churchend GL2 52 B1
Churchfield Rd GL4 31 E3
Churchfields GL52 8 D2
Churchill Cl GL6 48 B4
Churchill Dr GL52 17 E1
Churchill Gdns GL52 17 E1
Churchill Ind Est GL53 16 C3
Churchill Rd, Brimscombe GL5 45 H5
Churchill Rd, Cheltenham GL53 16 C3
Churchill Rd, Gloucester GL1 24 C4
Churchill Rd, Nailsworth GL6 48 B4
Churchill Wy GL6 35 F2
Churchlands Flats GL54 7 B6

Churchview Dr GL4 26 A3
Churhfield Rd GL5 41 E6
Churn Av GL52 13 E4
Churn Cl GL7 66 D2
Cirencester Bsns Centre GL7 61 F5
Cirencester Hospital GL7 60 D4
Cirencester Rd, Chalford GL6 47 F6
Cirencester Rd, Cheltenham GL53 17 E2
Cirencester Rd, Cirencester GL7 65 E1
Cirencester Rd, Gloucester GL3 32 D3
Cirencester Rd, Minchinhampton GL6 49 E1
Cirencester Rd, Tetbury GL8 57 D3
City Bank Rd GL7 61 F5
Clapham Ct GL1 4 E1
Clare Ct GL5 41 E5
Clare Pl GL53 16 B2
Clare St, Cheltenham GL53 16 B2
Clare St, Gloucester GL1 4 B1
Claremont Ct GL1 4 F2
Claremont Rd GL1 4 F2
Clarence Ct GL52 5 D1
Clarence Gate GL50 5 C2
Clarence Par GL50 5 B4
Clarence Rd, Cheltenham GL52 5 C2
Clarence Rd, Wotton-under-Edge GL12 56 D3
Clarence Sq GL50 5 C2
Clarence St, Cheltenham GL50 5 B3
Clarence St, Gloucester GL1 4 D3
Clarence Walk GL1 4 D3
Clarendon Ct GL5 6 C4
Clarendon Rd GL54 7 A4
Claridge Cl GL4 30 D1
Clarington Mews GL50 5 C1
Clarke Wy GL50 5 A1
Clarkes Cl GL5 45 G5
Clarkia Cl GL3 22 C2
Clarks Hay GL7 66 D2
Clarks La GL7 64 A3
Clarrie Rd GL8 57 D1
Claudians Cl GL4 26 B5
Clayburn Cl GL2 7 C1
Clayfurlong Gro GL7 68 B2
Claypits La GL6 45 F2
Claypits Path GL53 16 D3
Clearwater Dr GL2 28 A4
Cleeve Bsns Pk GL52 8 B4
Cleeve Cloud La GL52 13 H3
Cleeve Ct GL52 8 D3
Cleeve Lake Ct GL52 8 B2
Cleeve Rd GL4 30 B1
Cleeve View Rd GL52 13 E5
Cleeve Vw GL52 13 F5
Cleevecroft Av GL52 8 D3
Cleeveland St GL51 12 A4
Cleevelands Av GL50 12 C2
Cleevelands Cl GL50 12 C2
Cleevelands Dr GL50 12 C2
Cleevemont GL52 12 C2
Cleevemount Cl GL52 12 D3
Cleevemount Rd GL52 13 E3
Clegram Rd GL1 24 C4
Clematis Ct GL52 8 C3
Clement St GL1 25 F4
Clevedon Rd GL1 25 E5
Clevedon Sq GL51 15 G1
Clifton Rd GL1 24 C4
Clomoney Wy GL2 22 A4
Close Gdns GL8 57 C3
Clover Dr GL2 33 C1
Clover Piece GL4 26 A5
Clyde Cres GL52 13 E4
Clyde Rd GL3 32 C2
Coach House Mews GL7 61 E3
Coates Gdns GL10 38 D4
Coates Ho GL51 15 F1
Coberley Rd, Cheltenham GL51 15 E3
Coberley Rd, Gloucester GL4 29 G3
Cobham Rd GL51 12 A3
Coburn Gdns GL51 14 D2
Cochran Cl GL3 23 E4
Cockerell Rd GL2 33 F2

Cold Pool La GL51 14 C6
Coldray Cl GL1 25 G2
Coldwell GL10 43 E3
Coldwell Cl GL10 43 E3
Coldwell La GL10 43 E4
Cole Av GL2 28 D2
Colebridge Av GL2 21 H6
Colerne Dr GL3 27 E4
Colesbourne Rd GL51 16 C1
Colin Rd GL4 25 H2
College Baths Rd GL53 16 C1
College Ct GL1 4 C2
College Gate GL53 16 D1
College Grn GL1 4 C2
College Lawn GL53 16 C2
College Rd,
  Cheltenham GL53 5 C6
College Rd, Stroud GL5 40 B4
College St GL1 4 C2
College Vw,
  Cirencester GL7 60 D6
College Vw,
  Stonehouse GL10 38 D5
Colletts Dr GL51 12 A3
Colliers Wood GL6 48 A4
Collingbourne Rd GL4 25 F5
Collum End Rise GL53 16 B5
Colne Av GL52 13 E4
Coltham Cl GL52 17 E1
Coltham Flds GL52 12 D6
Coltham Rd GL52 17 E1
Coltishall Cl GL2 28 C5
Coltman Cl GL1 25 G2
Columbia Cl GL1 4 E1
Columbia St GL2 12 C5
Colville Ho GL7 61 E3
Colwell Av GL3 26 C2
Colwell School Cl GL1 25 F3
Colwyn Dr GL51 15 F5
Colyberry Rd GL52 9 E2
Combers End GL8 57 C2
Combrook Cl GL4 31 E1
Commercial Rd,
  Gloucester GL1 4 B3
Commercial Rd,
  Stroud GL6 40 B4
Commercial St GL50 16 B1
Common Ho GL5 6 D2
Common Rd GL6 48 D3
Compton Cl GL3 22 C1
Compton Rd GL51 12 A3
Concorde Wy GL4 25 G4
Conduit St GL1 25 E4
Coney Hill Par GL4 25 H4
Coney Hill Rd GL4 25 G4
Coniston Rd,
  Cheltenham GL51 15 F4
Coniston Rd,
  Gloucester GL2 21 H5
Constance Cl GL5 44 A1
Constitution Walk GL1 4 C3
Convent La GL4 44 A6
Conway Rd GL3 26 D4
Conygar Rd GL8 57 C1
Cooks Orch GL1 21 F6
Cookspool GL8 57 C1
Coombe Glen La GL51 15 E5
Coombe La,
  Stonehouse GL10 43 F4
Coombe La,
  Wotton-under-Edge
  GL12 56 F2
Coombe Mead GL52 9 E3
Coombe Rd GL12 56 E2
Coombe Ter GL12 56 E1
Coopers Ct GL3 32 C2
Coopers Elm GL2 28 C3
Coopers Pitch GL5 45 E4
Coopers Vw GL3 32 C3
Copper Beech Gro GL2 28 B4
Copper Cl GL52 9 F2
Copperfield Cl GL4 30 B1
Coppice Gate GL51 11 F4
Coppice Hill GL6 47 E4
Coppice Mews GL3 26 D4
Copt Elm Cl GL53 17 E2
Copt Elm Rd GL53 17 E3
Coral Cl GL4 29 E3
Cordingley Cl GL3 23 E5
Corfe Cl GL52 13 G3
Coriander Dr GL3 22 C3
Corinium Av GL4 25 H2
Corinium Centre GL7 61 F6
Corinium Gate GL7 61 E3
Corinium Ho GL7 60 C4
Corncroft La GL4 30 C3
Corner La GL11 53 G5

Cornfield Dr,
  Cheltenham GL52 8 B1
Cornfield Dr,
  Gloucester GL2 33 C1
Cornflower Rd GL4 26 A6
Cornhill GL5 6 C4
Cornmeadow Dr GL51 11 E4
Cornwall Av GL51 15 G1
Corolin Rd GL2 28 D2
Coronation Gro GL2 25 G1
Coronation Rd,
  Cheltenham GL52 13 F3
Coronation Rd,
  Stroud GL5 6 A6
Coronation Rd,
  Tetbury GL8 57 C1
Coronation Sq GL51 15 E1
Corpus St GL52 12 D6
Cossack Ct GL6 48 B5
Cotswold Av,
  Cirencester GL7 60 D5
Cotswold Av,
  Stonehouse GL10 37 B5
Cotswold Cl,
  Cirencester GL7 60 D4
Cotswold Cl, Stroud GL5 45 H5
Cotswold Cl, Tetbury GL8 57 D1
Cotswold Community
  GL7 67 A5
Cotswold Edge Bsns Pk
  GL2 24 B3
Cotswold Gdns,
  Gloucester GL2 22 A4
Cotswold Gdns,
  Wotton-under-Edge
  GL12 56 E3
Cotswold Grn GL10 38 D4
Cotswold Mead GL6 35 F3
Cotswold Rd,
  Cheltenham GL52 13 E3
Cotswold Rd,
  Stroud GL5 39 H4
Cotswold Vw,
  Cheltenham GL52 13 F5
Cotswold Vw,
  Gloucester GL2 24 A5
Cotswold Vw,
  Woodmancote GL52 9 E3
Cotswold Wy,
  Cheltenham GL52 9 H4
Cotswold Wy,
  Stroud GL6 35 E2
Cottage Fld GL2 7 B1
Cottage Gdns GL6 48 A3
Cottage Rake Av GL50 12 A2
Cotteswold Rd GL4 25 F6
Cotteswold Rise GL5 41 E5
Cotton Cl GL4 31 F1
Cottons La GL8 8 D3
Countess Lilias Rd GL7 60 D5
County Court Rd GL50 5 C4
County Cres GL1 25 F2
Court Gdn GL11 51 A6
Court Gdns GL2 24 A5
Court Mdw GL12 56 E2
Court Mews GL52 17 E2
Court Orch GL12 56 E3
Court Pl GL4 25 H5
Court Rd,
  Cheltenham GL53 13 G3
Court Rd,
  Gloucester GL3 32 B2
Court Vw, Chalford GL6 47 F3
Court Vw,
  Stonehouse GL10 38 B5
Court Wy GL5 44 B1
Courtenay St GL50 5 C1
Courtfield GL8 57 C2
Courtfield Dr GL52 17 F3
Courtfield Rd GL2 28 B5
Courthouse Gdns GL11 54 C2
Courtiers Dr GL52 8 D3
Cousley Cl GL3 26 D5
Cove House Gdns SN6 67 C7
Cow La GL5 48 A2
Cowcombe Hill GL6 47 E5
Cowl La GL54 7 B5
Cowle Rd GL5 41 E6
Cowley Cl GL51 15 E4
Cowley La GL4 29 G3
Cowlsmead GL51 18 C3
Cowper Rd GL51 15 E2
Cowslip Mdw GL52 9 E3
Cowswell La GL6 46 A3
Coxmore Cl GL3 26 D4
Coxs Hill SN6 67 C6
Coxs Wy GL4 26 C6

Coxwell Ct GL7 60 D3
Coxwell St GL7 60 D3
Crabtree La GL7 61 G4
Crabtree Pl GL50 12 B3
Cranford Cl GL52 9 F3
Cranham Cl GL4 31 E1
Cranham La GL3 23 F6
Cranham Rd GL52 12 D6
Cranhams La GL7 60 C5
Cranwell Cl GL4 30 B2
Craven Dr GL3 22 D3
Crawley Hill GL11 51 C4
Credon Rd GL3 26 B2
Crescent Cl GL10 38 B6
Crescent Pl GL50 5 B4
Crescent Rd GL10 38 B6
Crescent Ter GL50 5 B4
Crescentdale GL2 21 F3
Crest Wy GL4 26 B2
Cricklade Rd GL7 61 G5
Cricklade St GL7 61 E3
Criftycraft La GL3 23 F6
Cripps Rd GL7 60 D3
Crispin Cl,
  Cheltenham GL54 7 B4
Crispin Cl,
  Gloucester GL2 21 H4
Crispin Rd GL54 7 B4
Crock Mead GL4 26 A6
Croft Av GL53 17 F4
Croft Cl GL3 23 F5
Croft Dr GL53 17 E4
Croft Gdns GL53 17 F4
Croft La GL53 16 B2
Croft Mews GL53 17 E4
Croft Par GL53 17 E4
Croft Rd GL53 17 E4
Croft St GL53 16 B3
CroftThorne Cl GL51 15 F5
Cromwell Rd GL52 13 E4
Cromwell St GL1 4 D4
CromwellTer GL5 44 A2
Crosby Cl GL3 26 D5
Cross Keys La GL1 4 C3
Crowfield GL52 9 F2
Crown Cl GL52 8 D3
Crown Ct GL10 42 D3
Crown Dr GL52 8 C3
Crucis Park Farm Cotts
  GL7 62 D1
Crypt Ct GL4 29 E2
Crythan Walk GL51 15 G6
Cuckoo Cl GL6 46 C3
Cuckoo Row GL6 49 F2
Cud La GL6 34 C2
Cudnall St GL53 17 E2
Culver Hill GL5 44 B6
Culross Cl GL50 12 C2
Culverhay GL12 56 D2
Cumberland Cres GL51 15 G2
Cummings Ct GL2 13 E2
Curlew Rd GL4 25 G5
Curtis Hayward Dr GL2 28 B4
Cutham La GL7 58 D1
Cutler Rd GL5 41 E4
Cutsdean Cl GL52 8 B2
Cutwell GL8 57 C4

Daffodil Cl GL4 26 A6
Daffodil Leaze GL10 43 E4
Dagmar Rd GL50 16 A2
Dainty St GL1 25 E4
Dairy Cl GL7 64 D1
Dairy Fm SN6 67 B8
Daisy Bank GL5 41 E6
Daisybank Rd GL53 16 C6
Dale Cl GL4 29 H1
Dale Walk GL52 8 D3
Dallaway GL5 45 F4
Dancers Hill GL4 26 A5
Dancey Rd GL3 22 C4
Dane Cl GL2 21 H4
Daniels Mdw GL2 28 D3
Daniels Trading Est GL5 44 A1
Dark La, Chalford GL6 46 C4
Dark La,
  Cheltenham GL51 11 H2
Dark La, Nailsworth GL6 44 A3
Dark La, Stroud GL5 44 C1
Darrett Cl GL2 28 B6
Dart Cl GL2 28 B3
Dart Rd GL52 13 F4
Darwin Cl GL51 14 D2
Darwin Rd GL4 30 A1
Davallia Dr GL51 15 G6

Davey Cl GL2 33 D1
David French Ct GL51 15 H6
Dawson Cl GL4 31 E1
Dawson Glade GL53 17 E4
Daylesford Cl GL51 15 E3
Deacons Pl GL52 8 C4
Deakin Cl GL51 11 H2
Deans Cl GL51 15 G4
Deans Quarry GL5 49 F1
Deans Row GL1 20 D5
Deans Ter GL1 20 D6
Deans Walk GL1 4 C1
Deans Wy,
  Cheltenham GL52 8 D3
Deans Wy,
  Gloucester GL1 20 D6
Decon Cl GL51 15 G4
Deep St GL52 13 F2
Deer Park Rd GL3 26 C2
Deerhurst Cl GL4 31 E1
Deerhurst Pl GL2 28 A4
Dehaviland Rd GL52 8 C5
Delabere Rd GL52 8 D4
Delancey Hospital
  GL53 16 C4
Delaford Rd GL54 7 B5
Delkin Rd GL11 54 B3
Delmont Gro GL5 6 C1
Delphinium Dr GL52 8 B3
Delta Wy GL3 32 A2
Denbigh Rd GL51 15 F5
Denham Cl,
  Cheltenham GL51 9 F3
Denham Cl,
  Gloucester GL4 29 E4
Denley Cl GL52 8 D3
Denmark Ct GL1 21 F6
Denmark Rd GL1 21 E6
DentsTer GL54 7 B6
Derby Ct GL1 25 F3
Derby Rd GL1 25 F3
Derwent Cl GL3 32 C2
Derwent Walk GL51 15 F4
Desford Cl GL4 31 F1
Detmore Cl GL53 17 G3
Devereaux Cres GL5 39 F6
Devereaux Rd GL5 39 F6
Devon Av GL51 15 G2
DevonaTer GL5 39 G4
Devonshire St GL50 5 A3
Dewey Cl GL51 9 E3
Dianas Cl GL4 26 C5
Dickens Cl GL4 25 E6
Digby Green GL2 28 C5
Dill Av GL51 11 F5
Dimore Cl GL2 28 A6
Dinas Cl GL51 15 F5
Dinas Rd GL51 15 F5
Dinely St GL1 25 E3
Dinglewell GL3 26 C4
Discovery Rd GL4 26 C6
Distel Cl GL50 12 A1
Doctor Newtons Wy GL5 6 A4
Dodington Cl GL4 26 A4
Dog Bark La GL51 11 F1
Dollar St GL7 60 D2
Donside GL7 58 C6
Dora Walk GL1 25 E5
Dorchester Ct*,
  Moorend Park Rd GL53 16 A3
Dorington Ct GL6 46 B2
Dormer Rd GL11 11 G5
Dorney Rd GL1 24 D5
Dorrincourt Mews GL50 12 A5
Dorrit Cl GL51 25 E5
Dorset Av GL51 15 G1
Douro Rd GL50 12 A6
Doverdale Dr GL2 22 A5
Doverhay GL51 15 F5
Dowding Wy GL3 23 E4
Dowers La GL7 58 A1
Down Vw GL8 46 D3
Downfield GL5 40 A4
Downfield Ho GL5 18 B3
Downfield Rd GL5 40 A5
Downham Vw GL11 55 F7
Downs Wy GL7 59 E3
Downton Rd GL10 38 C6
Downy Cl GL2 28 A4
Dowty Ho GL50 5 C2
Dowty Rd GL51 15 F1
Dozule Cl GL10 42 C3
Drake Cl GL3 22 C2
Drake Ho GL50 12 A6
Drake La GL11 55 E6
Drakes Pl GL50 12 A6
Drapers Ct GL52 9 E3

Draycott Bsns Pk GL11
Draycott Cres GL11
Draycott Rd GL51
Drayton Cl GL51
Drayton Wy GL4
Drews Cl GL3
Drews Ct GL3
Drift Cl GL7
Drift Wy GL7
Drive Browns Cl GL6
Drive Browns Rd GL6
Drive Crawfords Cl GL6
Drive Crouchs Rd GL6
Drive Middletons Rd GL6
Drivemoor GL4
Druids La GL4
Druids Oak GL2
Dry Meadow La GL3
Dryland Mews GL3
Dryleaze GL12
Dryleaze Ct GL12
Dryleaze Gdns GL12
Ducie St GL1
Duckworth Cl GL53
Dudbridge Hill GL5
Dudbridge Mdw GL5
Dudbridge Rd GL5
Duderstadt Cl GL5
Dudley Fm GL7
Dugdale Rd GL7
Duke of Beaufort Ct GL
Duke St GL52
Dumbleton Gro GL51
Dunalley Par GL50
Dunalley St GL50
Dunbar Cl GL51
Duncourt Cotts GL7
Duncroft Rd GL3
Dunkirk Pitch GL6
Dunlin Cl GL2
Dunstan Glen GL3
Dunster Cl,
  Cheltenham GL51
Dunster Cl,
  Gloucester GL4
Dunster Gdns GL51
Dunster Gro GL51
Dunster Rd GL51
Durand Cl GL2
Durand Ct GL12
Durham Cl GL51
Durham Rd GL4
Dursley Rd,
  Dursley GL11
Dursley Rd,
  Gloucester GL2
Dyer St GL7
Dynevor St GL1

Eagle Cl GL6
Eagle Mill Cl GL5
Eagle Wy GL4
Eardisland Rd GL4
East Approach Dr GL52
East Court Mews GL52
East Court Villa GL52
East Ct GL53
East Dr GL5
East End Rd GL53
East Gable GL52
Eastbrook Rd GL4
Eastbrook Trading Est
  GL4
Eastcombe Rd GL4
Eastcott Wy GL3
Eastern Av GL4
Eastern Av Retail Pk GL4
Eastfield SN6
Eastfield Mews GL4
Eastfld Rd GL6
Eastgate Shopping Cent
  GL1
Eastgate St GL1
Eastington Mews GL10
Eastington
  Trading Est GL10
Eastville Cl GL4
Eaton Pl GL53
Ebley By-Pass GL10
Ebley Rd GL10
Ebor Rd GL2
Eccles Ct GL8
Eddison Cl GL2
Edendale App GL51
Edendale Rd GL51
Edge La GL6
Edge Rd GL6

73

75

Limekiln Gro GL2   7 B1
Limes Cl GL7   60 D5
Limes Rd GL7   68 B3
Linacre Cres GL7   60 C6
Lincoln Av GL51   15 G6
Linden Av GL52   13 E2
Linden Cl GL52   13 F2
Linden Rd GL1   24 C4
Lindhurst Cl GL52   9 E2
Lindley Chase GL52   8 B2
Linfoot Rd GL8   57 B3
Links Vw GL7   58 D4
Linnet Cl GL4   25 G6
Linsley Wy GL4   29 F4
Linton Cl GL53   16 C2
Linwell Cl GL50   12 A1
Linworth Rd GL52   9 E3
Lion Cl GL2   28 B3
Lipson Rd GL51   11 F5
Lisle Mews GL52   5 D1
Lisle Pl GL12   56 B2
Lister St GL11   55 E6
Little Acorns GL52   8 B1
Little Acre GL12   56 B2
Little Bayshill Ter GL50   5 A4
Little Cleevemount GL52   12 D3
Little Elmbridge GL2   22 A5
Little Herberts Cl GL53   17 F4
Little Herberts Rd GL53   17 F4
Little Hills Cotts GL51   18 D3
Little Lancarridge GL2   7 B2
Little Normans GL2   21 H4
Little Orch GL52   8 C2
Little Walk GL2   21 H4
Littlecote Cl GL52   8 B3
Littledown Rd GL53   16 D5
Littlefield GL2   28 B4
Llandilo St GL1   24 C4
Llanthony Ind Est GL2   *24 B2*
Llanthony Rd GL2   4 A4
Llanthony Warehouse
GL1   *4 A4*
Lloyd Barber Ct*,
  Cornfield Dr GL2   33 C1
Lloyd Cl GL51   15 E1
Lobb Court GL1   25 F2
Lobleys Dr GL4   26 B6
Locking Hill GL5   6 C2
Locombe Pl GL12   56 E4
Lodgemore Cl GL5   40 B5
Lodgemore La GL5   40 B5
London Ho GL1   25 E1
London Pl GL7   61 F3
London Rd,
  Brimscombe GL5   45 E1
London Rd,
  Chalford GL6   46 A5
London Rd,
  Cheltenham GL52   5 D5
London Rd,
  Cirencester GL7   61 F3
London Rd,
  Gloucester GL1   4 E2
London Rd, Stroud GL5   6 C4
London Rd, Tetbury GL8   57 C2
Long Mynd Av GL51   15 E5
Long St, Dursley GL11   55 E6
Long St, Tetbury GL8   57 C3
Long St,
  Wotton-under-Edge
  GL12   56 D3
Longaston Cl GL2   52 B1
Longaston La GL2   52 B1
Longborough Dr GL4   31 E1
Longfield GL2   28 B4
Longford La GL2   21 E3
Longford Mews GL2   21 E3
Longfurlong La GL8   57 A4
Longhope Cl GL4   26 B6
Longland Ct GL2   21 G5
Longland Gdns GL2   21 G5
Longlands Cl GL52   9 E2
Longlands Rd GL52   9 E3
Longleat Av GL4   29 E4
Longlength La GL6   51 D2
Longney Rd GL4   29 F2
Longsmith St GL1   4 B2
Longtree Cl GL8   57 C1
Longville Cl GL4   26 B6
Longway Av GL53   17 F4
Lonsdale Rd GL2   25 H1
Loriners Cl GL2   28 B4
Lovage Cl GL3   22 C3
Love La, Cirencester GL7   61 E5
Love La, Stroud GL5   45 G6
Love La, Tetbury GL8   57 D3
Love Lane Ind Est GL7   *61 F6*

Lovedays Mead GL5   6 B1
Lower Churchfield Rd
  GL5   41 E6
Lower Dorrington Ter GL5   6 D5
Lower Kitesnest La GL6   34 B6
Lower Leazes GL5   40 D5
Lower Mdw GL2   28 B6
Lower Mill St GL51   12 A4
Lower Newmarket Rd
  GL6   48 A4
Lower Poole Rd GL11   55 E7
Lower Quay St GL1   4 B2
Lower Spillmans GL5   40 B6
Lower St,
  Ruscombe GL6   40 A1
Lower St, Stroud GL5   6 D4
Lower Tuffley La GL2   28 D2
Lower Washwell La GL6   35 G1
Lower Wharf GL5   6 A4
Lower Wharf Ind Est GL5   *6 A4*
Loweswater Cl GL5   15 G4
Loweswater Rd GL51   15 G4
Lowfield Rd GL8   57 C2
Lucinda Mews GL51   11 G6
Ludgate Hill GL12   56 D3
Luke La GL3   22 B3
Lye La GL52   9 G5
Lyfield Cl GL53   17 F3
Lyfield Rd East GL53   17 E3
Lyfield Rd West GL53   17 E3
Lygon Walk GL51   11 G5
Lynch Rd GL6   47 E3
Lyncroft Farm Workshops
GL7   *58 C1*
Lyndale Ter GL51   15 H1
Lyneham Dr GL2   28 D5
Lyng Cl GL4   26 B4
Lynmouth Rd GL3   26 C5
Lynton Rd GL3   26 C5
Lynworth Pl GL52   13 E3
Lynworth Ter GL52   13 F3
Lypiatt Dr GL50   16 A1
Lypiatt La GL50   16 A1
Lypiatt Mews GL50   16 A1
Lypiatt Rd GL50   16 A1
Lypiatt St GL50   16 A1
Lypiatt Ter GL50   16 A1
Lypiatt Vw GL6   46 B2
Lysander Ct GL2   23 E4
Lysons Av GL1   24 C4

Mackenzie Wy GL51   11 G3
Madleaze Ind Est GL1   *24 C4*
Madleaze Rd GL1   24 C4
Magdala Rd GL1   25 F3
Magdalen Rd GL8   57 C2
Magnolia Ct GL51   14 D1
Magnolia Walk GL2   28 B6
Magpie Cl GL10   38 C4
Maida Vale Rd GL53   16 B3
Maidenhall GL2   7 B1
Main Rd GL6   40 A1
Mainard Sq GL2   21 G4
Maisemore Rd GL2   20 A2
Malden Rd GL52   5 D2
Maldon Gdns GL1   25 E5
Malet Cl GL2   21 H4
Mallard Cl GL2   28 A4
Malmesbury Rd,
  Cheltenham GL51   11 G4
Malmesbury Rd,
  Gloucester GL4   25 F4
Malthouse La,
  Cheltenham GL50   5 B1
Malthouse La,
  Winchcombe GL54   7 A6
Malthouse Walk GL8   57 C2
Malvern Gdns GL5   39 H5
Malvern Pl GL50   12 A6
Malvern Rd,
  Cheltenham GL50   15 H1
Malvern Rd,
  Gloucester GL1   21 E5
Malvern St GL51   12 A4
Malvern View Bsns Pk
GL52   *8 A2*
Manchester Pk GL51   11 H5
Mandara Gro GL4   30 D1
Mandarin Wy GL50   12 A1
Mandeville Cl GL2   21 H4
Mankley Rd GL10   42 C3
Manley Gdns GL2   21 H4
Manor Av GL11   54 B2
Manor Cl,
  Cirencester GL7   58 C5
Manor Cl, Dursley GL11   54 B1
Manor Cl, Stroud GL6   49 F2

Manor Ct,
  Cheltenham GL51   11 H2
Manor Ct,
  Gloucester GL4   30 B1
Manor Dr GL5   44 B5
Manor Gdns,
  Gloucester GL4   26 B3
Manor Gdns, Stroud GL5   44 B5
Manor La GL12   56 D2
Manor Park Bsns Centre
GL51   *11 G3*
Manor Pk,
  Cheltenham GL51   15 E5
Manor Pk,
  Gloucester GL2   22 A5
Manor Rd GL51   11 G4
Manse Gdns GL51   15 G4
Mansell Cl GL2   24 B6
Manser St GL50   12 B3
Mansfield Av GL2   29 E1
Mansfield Mews GL2   28 C6
Maple Cl, Dursley GL11   54 D4
Maple Cl,
  Gloucester GL2   28 A6
Maple Ct GL2   22 A5
Maple Dr,
  Cheltenham GL53   17 F4
Maple Dr,
  Gloucester GL3   32 A1
Maple Dr, Stroud GL5   40 B3
Marchant Cl GL51   11 G5
Marchesi Walk GL12   56 E2
Marconi Dr GL2   33 E2
Marefield Cl GL4   26 C6
Margrett Rd GL50   12 B3
Marian Ct GL1   4 B1
Marjoram Cl GL4   26 C6
Market Par GL1   4 E2
Market Pl,
  Cirencester GL7   61 E5
Market Pl, Tetbury GL8   57 D3
Market Sq GL6   49 G2
Market St,
  Cheltenham GL50   12 A4
Market St, Stroud GL6   48 C5
Market St,
  Wotton-under-Edge
  GL12   56 D3
Market Wy GL1   4 D3
Marlborough Cl,
  Bishops Cleeve GL52   8 B3
Marlborough Cl,
  Cheltenham GL52   17 E2
Marlborough Cres GL4   25 F5
Marlborough Rd GL4   25 F5
Marle Hill GL6   46 D4
Marle Hill Par GL50   5 C1
Marle Hill Rd GL50   12 B3
Marley La GL6   47 F5
Marleyfield Cl GL3   22 C2
Marleyfield Wy GL3   22 C2
Marling Cl GL5   44 C6
Marling Cres GL5   40 A5
Marlstone Rd GL11   54 C3
Marment Rd GL11   54 A4
Marram Cl GL4   26 B4
Marsh Cl GL51   12 A3
Marsh Dr GL51   12 B3
Marsh Gdns GL51   12 B3
Marsh La,
  Cheltenham GL51   12 A3
Marsh La,
  Stonehouse GL10   42 C3
Marsh Mews GL10   42 C2
Marsh Rd GL10   42 C2
Marsh Ter GL51   18 C3
Marsh View GL10   42 C2
Marshalls Par GL5   5 C2
Marsland Rd GL51   11 E6
Marston Rd GL52   12 D2
Marten Cl GL4   26 C6
Martin Cl GL7   60 D5
Martindale Rd GL3   22 A4
Marwell Cl GL4   29 G5
Mary Godwin Ct GL51   11 G4
Mary Gro GL2   7 B1
Mary Rose Av GL3   22 C2
Masefield GL7   60 D5
Mason Rd GL5   41 F5
Massey Par GL1   25 F4
Massey Rd GL1   25 F4
Mathews Wy GL5   40 A4
Matson Av GL4   30 C1
Matson La GL4   30 B2
Matson Pl GL1   25 F5
Maverdine Ct GL1   4 B1
Maverdine Pass GL1   4 C2

May Ct GL50   12 A6
May Evans Cl GL11   54 B3
May La GL11   55 D7
May Tree Sq GL4   25 H5
Mayall Ct GL4   30 C3
Mayfair Cl GL2   24 B4
Mayfield Cl GL52   8 C4
Mayfield Dr GL3   26 C3
Mayhill Wy GL1   25 F1
Mays La GL8   50 B4
Maythorn Dr GL51   11 E5
Mead Cl GL53   16 C3
Mead Rd,
  Cheltenham GL53   16 B3
Mead Rd,
  Gloucester GL4   26 B6
Meade King Gro GL52   9 E3
Meadow Cl,
  Cheltenham GL51   14 C2
Meadow Cl,
  Cirencester GL7   61 E5
Meadow Ct GL10   38 C4
Meadow La GL51   15 F6
Meadow La West GL5   39 H6
Meadow Lea GL52   8 B4
Meadow Rd,
  Cirencester GL7   61 E5
Meadow Rd,
  Stonehouse GL10   38 C4
Meadow Vale GL11   54 B3
Meadow Vw,
  Cheltenham GL52   17 F1
Meadow Vw,
  Cirencester GL7   59 E4
Meadow Vw,
  Frampton on Severn
  GL2   36 A6
Meadow Wy,
  Gloucester GL3   22 D3
Meadow Wy,
  South Cerney GL7   66 C2
Meadow Wy,
  Stroud GL5   39 H6
Meadoway GL52   8 B4
Meadowcroft GL4   26 B6
Meadowleaze GL2   21 H6
Meadowsweet Walk GL2   28 D4
Meads Cl GL52   8 D3
Meadvale Cl GL2   21 H6
Meadway Rd GL10   38 C6
Medoc Cl GL50   12 A2
Medway Cres GL3   32 D2
Meerstone Wy GL4   30 D2
Melbourne Cl,
  Cheltenham GL53   16 A3
Melbourne Cl,
  Stonehouse GL10   38 C3
Melbourne Dr GL10   38 C3
Melbourne St East GL1   25 E4
Melbourne St West GL1   25 E4
Meldon Ter GL5   6 B3
Melick Cl GL4   30 D1
Melmore Gdns GL7   61 F5
Melody Wy GL2   22 A4
Melville Rd GL3   22 D4
Mendip Cl,
  Cheltenham GL52   13 E3
Mendip Cl,
  Gloucester GL2   28 A5
Mendip Ho GL52   13 E3
Mendip Rd GL52   13 E3
Merchants Mead GL2   28 A4
Merchants Quay Shopping
Centre GL1   *4 A3*
Merchants Rd GL2   4 A4
Mercia GL1   20 D6
Mercia Rd GL54   7 A5
Mercian Cl GL7   61 F5
Mercian Ct GL50   16 A2
Mercury Wy GL4   26 C5
Merestones Cl GL50   16 A3
Merestones Dr GL50   15 H3
Merestones Rd GL50   15 H5
Merevale Rd GL2   25 G1
Merlin Cl GL53   16 A3
Merlin Dr GL2   28 A4
Merlin Haven GL12   56 C3
Merlin Wy GL4   26 C5
Merretts Mill Ind Centre
GL5   *48 A1*
Merretts Orch GL2   52 B2
Merriville Gdns GL51   11 G6
Merriville Rd GL51   11 G6
Merrywalk Shopping Centre
GL5   *6 B3*
Merrywalks GL5   6 A3
Mersey Rd GL52   13 E5

Merton Cl GL10
Meteor Bsns Pk GL3
Meteor Ct GL4
Meteor Wy GL3
Metz Wy GL1
Michaelmas Ct GL1
Michaels Mead GL7
Mickle Mead,
  Gloucester GL4
Mickle Mead,
  Highnam GL2
Middle Cft GL4
Middle Hay Ct GL52
Middle Hill, Bussage GL6
Middle Hill, Stroud GL6
Middle Hill Cres GL6
Middle Leazes GL5
Middle Rd GL5
Middle Spillmans GL5
Middle St, Stroud GL5
Middle St, Uplands GL5
Middle Tynings GL6
Middlecroft GL10
Middleton Lawn GL3
Midland Rd,
  Cirencester GL7
Midland Rd,
  Gloucester GL1
Midland Rd,
  Stonehouse GL10
Midway GL6
Midwinter Av GL51
Midwinter Cl GL50
Mildenhall Way GL2
Mildreds Farm Barns
  GL7
Mildreds Fm GL7
Miles Rd GL2
Milford Cl GL2
Mill Cl,
  Cheltenham GL52
Mill Cl,
  South Cerney GL7
Mill Cl, Wotton-under-E
  GL12
Mill Cnr GL3
Mill Farm Dr GL5
Mill Gro GL2
Mill House Dr GL50
Mill La,
  Charlton Kings GL52
Mill La, Gloucester GL3
Mill La, Prestbury GL52
Mill La, Tetbury GL8
Mill La, Winchcombe G
Mill Pl GL7
Mill Pl Trading Est Nort
GL1
Mill Pl Trading Est Sout
GL2
Mill Pond End GL5
Mill Row GL10
Mill St,
  Cheltenham GL52
Mill St, Gloucester GL1
Mill Vw, Cirencester GL
Mill Vw, Stroud GL6
Millbank GL11
Millbridge Rd GL3
Millbrook Cl GL1
Millbrook Gdns GL51
Millbrook Pl GL5
Millbrook St,
  Cheltenham GL50
Millbrook St,
  Gloucester GL1
Millend La GL10
Millennium Wy GL7
Miller Cl GL2
Millers Grn GL1
Millfields GL3
Millham Rd GL52
Millin Av GL4
Milling Cl SN6
Millway GL11
Milne Walk GL51
Milo Pl GL1
Milsom St GL50
Milton Av,
  Cheltenham GL51
Milton Av,
  Gloucester GL2
Milton Gro GL5
Milton Rd GL51
Mimosa Av GL51
Minerva Cl GL4
Minerva Ct GL7

v GL52 8 D3
Cl GL52 8 B2
Gdns GL4 26 B5
Wy GL3 22 C1
n Rd GL51 15 E3
sh GL12 56 D3
GL53 5 C6
GL51 10 D3
d GL6 48 A4
Cl GL3 31 E1
Cl GL4 31 E1
dw Trading Est 12 C2
 24 B4
Puzzle Cl GL5 39 H6
oft GL51 15 E2
Av GL50 5 C2
d Rd GL2 21 G4
nery Cl GL2 27 E5
nery Rd GL51 15 E5
ier Arc GL50 1 D4
ier Ct GL1 5 A6
ier Dr GL50 4 C4
ier Gro GL50 5 B6
ier Mews GL1 16 B1
ier Par GL50 24 D3
ier Spa Rd GL50 5 B6
ier St GL50 5 A6
ier Ter GL50 5 A6
ier Villas GL50 5 A6
ier Walk GL50 16 B1
ier Walk Prom 12 B6

Dr GL51 11 F6
rat GL5 45 E3
a GL6 47 F1
GL7 63 H4
ll Pk GL5 39 G3
ll Pl GL5 39 H4
on on Severn 36 B1
Gloucester GL1 25 E4
art Dr GL52 12 D4
d Cres GL53 16 B3
d Glade GL53 17 E3
d Gro GL53 16 B4
d La GL2 52 A3
d Mews GL53 16 B3
d Park Rd GL53 16 A3
d Rd,
n Kings GL53 16 D3
d Rd,
ham GL53 16 B4
d St GL53 16 B4
d Rd GL3 32 B2
Av GL51 11 H5
erace GL5 45 E2
ds Gro GL1 25 E6
ds Trading Est 24 C4
l Dr GL7 60 C6
Cl GL52 8 D3
St GL1 25 E4
s Dr*,
n Pl GL50 16 B2
s Dr GL53 17 F5
Av GL3 22 C4
side Cl GL52 13 G2
side Courtyard 13 G2
ton Dr GL53 16 B3
St GL1 25 E4
t GL51 15 G4
ill Cl GL51 12 A1
rch GL11 54 C2
r Rd GL2 21 G4
Cotts GL1 4 F4
st Cl GL4 39 H5
Cres GL5 39 H5
Rd GL5 39 H4
Dr GL3 22 C3
n Pl GL3 32 B2
head Dr GL3 22 A2
d Rd GL7 65 F2
Pleasant,
ster GL2 28 D5
leasant,
GL5 41 E6
Pleasant,
-under-Edge 56 E3
st,
ester GL7 60 D5
st,
ester GL1 4 B1

Mowberry Cl GL2 21 H4
Mulberry Cl,
Cheltenham GL52 13 G2
Mulberry Cl,
Gloucester GL2 28 A6
Mulberry Ct GL51 14 D1
Mulberry Gdns GL4 30 B2
Mullings Ct GL7 61 E2
Munday Cl GL6 46 B2
Munsley Gro GL4 30 C3
Murlow Apartments*,
Uley Rd GL11 55 F7
Murray Cl GL52 8 C1
Murvagh Cl GL53 16 C1
Muscroft Rd GL52 13 H3
Mutsilver Mews GL2 22 A4
Myers Rd GL1 25 F2
Myrtle Cl GL4 30 A1
Naas La GL2 28 C6
Nailsworth Mills
Waterside Pk GL6 48 C5
Nailsworth Ter GL50 5 A2
Napier St GL1 4 F4
Nasse Ct GL11 54 C2
Nastead La GL10 37 D4
Natton Cotts GL52 17 H1
Nature Close GL3 32 B3
Naunton Cres GL53 16 B2
Naunton La GL53 16 B2
Naunton Par GL53 16 B2
Naunton Park Cl GL53 16 C3
Naunton Park Rd GL53 16 C2
Naunton Rd GL4 25 H4
Naunton Ter GL53 16 B2
Naunton Wy GL53 16 B2
Needham Av GL2 33 E1
Nelmes Row GL52 17 G3
Nelson St,
Gloucester GL1 25 E5
Nelson St, Stroud GL5 39 H4
Nene Cl GL2 28 B3
Neptune Cl GL4 26 B5
Netheridge Cl GL2 28 C1
Netherwood Cl GL51 11 G6
Netherwood Gdns GL51 11 G6
Nettleton Rd,
Cheltenham GL51 15 E4
Nettleton Rd,
Gloucester GL1 4 E4
New Barn Av GL52 13 E2
New Barn Cl GL52 13 E2
New Barn La GL52 12 C2
New Church St GL8 57 F3
New Cut GL11 51 B5
New Inn La,
Gloucester GL1 4 D2
New Inn La, Tetbury GL8 50 A4
New Leaze Gdns GL8 57 B2
New Mills Trading Est
GL5 41 E4
New Rd,
Cheltenham GL52 9 F3
New Rd, Dursley GL11 54 B4
New Rd,
Minchinhampton GL6 49 F3
New Rd, Selsley GL5 43 H2
New Rd, Wotton-under-Edge
GL12 56 A3
New Rutland Ct GL50 5 B2
New St,
Charlton Kings GL53 17 F3
New St,
Cheltenham GL50 5 A3
New St, Gloucester GL1 24 D3
New St, Painswick GL6 35 F2
New St,
Stonehouse GL10 42 D3
Newark Rd GL1 24 B5
Newcombe Ct GL7 61 F3
Newcourt Pk GL53 17 E3
Newcourt Rd GL53 17 E3
Newland St GL1 25 E1
Newlands Vw GL52 8 D6
Newmarket Rd GL6 48 A4
Newnton Rd GL8 57 D3
Newstead Rd GL4 26 B3
Newton Av GL4 30 D2
Newton Cl GL51 15 F1
Newton Rd GL51 11 F6
Nicolson Cl GL3 22 B3
Nine Elms Rd GL2 22 A5
Niven Ct GL51 15 F1
Noak Rd GL3 27 F5
Noake Rd GL3 26 D4
Noel Lee Wy GL51 54 C2
Norbury Av GL4 30 B1

Norcote Cotts GL7 61 H2
Nordown Cl GL11 54 C3
Nordown Rd GL11 54 C3
Norfolk Av GL51 15 G1
Norfolk Ct GL1 4 B4
Norfolk Mews GL1 4 C4
Norfolk St GL1 4 B4
Normal Ter GL50 5 B2
Norman Ball Wy GL51 25 G2
Norman Hill Rd GL11 54 B3
Nortenham Cl GL52 8 B2
North Farm Rd GL7 61 G4
North Field Mews GL5 6 D1
North Hall Mews GL52 12 D5
North Hill Rd GL7 61 F6
North Home Rd GL7 61 G4
North Pl GL50 5 C3
North Rd GL1 21 E5
North Rd East GL51 14 B4
North Rd West GL51 14 B4
North St,
Cheltenham GL50 5 C3
North St,
Winchcombe GL54 7 B5
North Upton La GL4 26 B4
North Wy GL7 61 E3
Northbank Cl GL51 14 C4
Northbrook Rd GL4 25 H2
Northfield Cl GL8 57 E2
Northfield Pass GL5 5 C2
Northfield Rd,
Gloucester GL4 25 E6
Northfield Rd,
Tetbury GL8 57 D2
Northfield Sq GL52 25 E6
Northfield Ter GL50 5 C2
Northfields Rd GL6 48 B3
Northgate St GL1 4 C3
Northlands Wy GL8 57 D1
Northleaze GL8 57 D2
Northmoor La GL7 65 F5
Norton Cl GL54 7 B4
Norton Ridge GL4 48 A3
Nortonwood GL6 48 A3
Norwich Dr GL51 15 G5
Norwood Rd GL50 16 B2
Notgrove Cl,
Cheltenham GL51 15 F3
Notgrove Cl,
Gloucester GL4 29 E3
Notley Pl GL3 26 D4
Nottingham Rd GL52 8 C1
Nouncells Cross GL5 41 E5
Nourse Cl GL53 18 F1
Noverton Av GL52 13 H2
Noverton La GL52 13 G2
Nunnery La GL11 55 D8
Nunny Cl GL51 14 D2
Nursery Cl,
Cirencester GL7 61 F5
Nursery Cl, Stroud GL5 41 E6
Nursery Ter GL10 34 B3
Nursery Vw GL7 64 B3
Nut Cft GL4 25 G4
Nuthill GL4 31 F3
Nutley Av GL4 29 E3
Nutmeg Cl GL4 30 D2
Nympsfield Rd,
Gloucester GL4 29 F3
Nympsfield Rd,
Stroud GL6 48 A3

Oak Av GL52 17 E1
Oak Bank GL4 29 G2
Oak Dr, Dursley GL11 54 D4
Oak Dr, Gloucester GL3 32 B1
Oak Dr, Stroud GL5 6 A5
Oak Manor Dr GL52 13 E5
Oak Tree Cl GL2 33 B1
Oak Tree Gdn GL4 30 C2
Oak Tree Vw GL4 30 C3
Oak Wy,
South Cerney GL7 66 D3
Oak Wy,
Stonehouse GL10 38 D5
Oakbrook Dr GL51 14 D4
Oakcroft Cl GL4 30 D3
Oakdene GL51 15 H3
Oakfield Rd GL52 8 D2
Oakfield St GL50 16 A2
Oakhurst Cl GL3 22 C4
Oakhurst Rise GL52 17 E1
Oakland St GL53 13 E3
Oakland St GL53 17 E2
Oaklands GL7 64 A3
Oakleaze GL52 22 A6

Oakley Rd,
Cheltenham GL52 13 E6
Oakley Rd,
Cirencester GL7 60 D5
Oakridge GL2 7 B1
Oakridge Cl GL4 31 E1
Oakwood Dr GL3 26 C5
Oatfield GL2 28 B3
Oatfield Rd GL2 36 B2
Oatground GL12 56 E3
Obrien Rd GL51 11 G5
Ocker Hill GL6 39 H2
Ogbourne Ct GL2 22 B6
Okus Rd GL53 17 E4
Old Bath Rd GL53 16 D2
Old Brewery La GL8 57 C3
Old Bristol Rd GL6 48 B6
Old Cheltenham Rd GL2 21 H5
Old Common GL6 49 H1
Old Ct GL11 54 E4
Old Elmore La GL2 28 C3
Old Gloucester Rd GL51 10 A6
Old Hill GL8 50 B3
Old Horsley Rd GL6 48 B6
Old London Rd GL12 56 C2
Old Milbrook Ter GL50 12 A4
Old Mkt GL6 48 C5
Old Neighbourhood GL6 46 C4
Old Painswick Cl GL4 25 G5
Old Painswick Rd GL4 25 G5
Old Rd GL52 9 F6
Old Rectory Cl GL5 44 B1
Old Reddings Cl GL51 14 D4
Old Reddings Rd GL51 14 D4
Old Row GL51 25 E3
Old School Cl GL6 48 B4
Old Station Cl GL6 46 D5
Old Station Dr GL53 16 B3
Old Town GL12 56 D2
Old Tram Rd GL1 4 C4
Old Vicarage La GL7 68 B4
Oldacre Dr GL52 8 D1
Oldbury Cl GL51 11 E6
Oldbury Orch GL3 23 F5
Oldbury Rd GL51 11 E6
Oldends La GL10 38 A5
Oldends La Ind Est GL10 38 A4
Oldfield Cres GL51 15 F2
Olio La GL53 5 C6
Olive Gro GL11 55 C5
Ollney Rd GL6 49 F2
Olympus Park
Bsns Centre GL2 28 C3
Olympus Pk GL2 28 C3
Orchard Av GL51 11 F6
Orchard Cl,
Cirencester GL7 68 B3
Orchard Cl, Dursley GL11 54 C2
Orchard Cl,
Gloucester GL2 21 E4
Orchard Cl,
Hardwicke GL2 33 B1
Orchard Cl,
Leonard Stanley GL10 42 C2
Orchard Cl,
Middleyard GL10 43 F3
Orchard Cotts GL52 17 G2
Orchard Ct,
Stonehouse GL10 38 C5
Orchard Ct, Stroud GL6 35 F2
Orchard Dr GL3 23 F5
Orchard Fld GL8 50 A4
Orchard Ho GL7 61 E3
Orchard La GL5 45 F5
Orchard Leaze GL11 54 A3
Orchard Mead,
Nailsworth GL6 48 B4
Orchard Mead,
Painswick GL6 35 F2
Orchard Pk GL3 26 C6
Orchard Pl GL10 38 C5
Orchard Priors GL52 13 E6
Orchard Rd,
Bishops Cleeve GL52 8 C3
Orchard Rd,
Cheltenham GL52 8 B5
Orchard Rd,
Gloucester GL2 22 B5
Orchard Rd, Stroud GL5 39 F6
Orchard Rd,
Winchcombe GL54 7 A5
Orchard Rise GL11 54 C4
Orchard St GL12 56 D3
Orchard Vw,
Cheltenham GL51 15 H6
Orchard Vw,
Dursley GL11 54 C4

Orchard Vw,
Shurdington GL51 18 C3
Orchard Vw, Stroud GL5 44 B2
Orchard Wy,
Cheltenham GL51 11 F6
Orchard Wy,
Gloucester GL3 22 D2
Organs Alley GL1 4 E3
Oriel Rd GL50 5 B5
Oriole Wy GL4 25 H5
Ormond Pl GL50 5 B4
Ormond Ter GL50 5 B5
Orrisdale Ter GL53 5 D6
Osborne Av GL4 29 F4
Osborne Ho GL51 15 H4
Osier Cl GL4 30 A1
Osprey Cl GL4 26 A6
Osprey Dr GL10 38 C4
Osprey Rd GL53 16 A4
Osric Rd GL1 25 E5
Othello Cl GL51 15 F1
Otter Rd GL4 26 C6
Oval App GL2 36 B3
Over Causeway GL2 20 A6
Overbrook Cl GL4 25 H2
Overbrook Dr GL52 25 H2
Overbrook Rd GL2 28 A6
Overbury Rd GL1 25 F3
Overbury St GL53 17 E2
Overhill Rd GL7 58 C6
Overton Ct GL50 12 A5
Overton Park Rd GL50 12 A5
Overton Rd GL50 12 A5
Owl Cl GL4 26 A6
Owls End Rd GL52 9 E1
Oxbutts Ind Est GL52 9 E2
Oxford Ho GL7 61 E3
Oxford Par GL52 12 D6
Oxford Pass GL50 5 C3
Oxford Rd GL1 4 F1
Oxford St,
Cheltenham GL52 12 D6
Oxford St,
Gloucester GL1 4 F2
Oxford Ter GL1 4 F2
Oxford Wy GL51 15 G6
Oxleaze Cl GL8 57 C2
Oxleaze Rd GL8 57 C2
Oxmead Cl GL2 9 E2
Oxmoor GL4 30 D2
Oxstalls Dr GL2 21 F4
Oxstalls La GL2 21 G6
Oxstalls Wy GL2 21 G5
Paddock Gdns GL2 21 H4
Paddock Rise GL50 38 C5
Paddocks La GL50 12 C2
Padin Cl GL6 46 C2
Paganhill Est GL5 40 A4
Paganhill La GL5 40 A5
Paget Ho GL7 61 E3
Pagets Rd GL2 9 E4
Painswick Old Rd GL6 6 A1
Painswick Rd,
Brockworth GL3 32 C3
Painswick Rd,
Cheltenham GL50 16 A2
Painswick Rd,
Gloucester GL4 25 F4
Painswick Rd,
Stroud GL6 6 A1
Palmer Av GL4 26 B6
Palmers Ct GL50 38 C5
Pampas Ct GL2 28 D3
Parabola Cl GL50 12 B6
Parabola La GL50 5 A5
Parabola Rd GL50 5 A5
Paragon Ter GL53 16 C1
Park Av GL2 21 H4
Park Brake GL2 7 B2
Park Cl GL8 57 D2
Park Ct GL5 41 E6
Park Dr GL2 28 B4
Park End SN6 67 D8
Park End Rd GL5 39 H3
Park Gate GL50 16 A2
Park Ho GL50 16 A2
Park La,
Cheltenham GL52 13 F1
Park La, Cirencester GL7 60 D3
Park La, Dursley GL11 55 A7
Park La, Nailsworth GL5 48 A2
Park Mews GL53 16 A3
Park Par GL10 38 B4
Park Pl,
Cheltenham GL52 16 A2
Park Pl, Swindon SN6 67 C8

79

Somerset Av,
   Dursley GL11   55 E8
Somerset Pass GL50   5 A4
Somerset Pl GL1   24 C3
Somerville Ct GL7   60 D6
Somme Rd GL52   13 F4
Soren Larsen Wy GL2   24 B5
Sorrel Cl GL4   30 A1
Southgate St GL1   4 B4
South Cerney Rd GL7   64 C1
South Cl GL2   21 G6
South St GL11   51 B5
South Vw,
   Stonehouse GL10   43 F3
South Vw, Stroud GL5   39 G6
South Wy GL7   61 E3
Southam La GL52   8 C6
Southam Rd GL52   13 G1
Southbank,
   Cheltenham GL51   11 G6
Southbank, Stroud GL5   44 A4
Southbrook Rd GL4   25 G2
Southcourt Dr GL53   16 B3
Southern Av GL4   29 G2
Southern Rd GL53   16 C5
Southfield, Stroud GL6   49 F2
Southfield, Tetbury GL8   57 C4
Southfield App GL53   16 D5
Southfield Cl GL53   16 C5
Southfield Rd,
   Gloucester GL4   29 H1
Southfield Rd,
   Stroud GL5   44 B4
Southfield Rise GL53   16 C5
Southgate Cres GL5   44 B1
Southgate Dr GL53   16 D1
Southgate Gdns GL5   44 B1
Southgate Mews GL7   61 F4
Southgate St GL1   24 C3
Southmead GL7   61 F5
Southview Wy GL52   13 G3
Southwood La GL50   16 A1
Spa Ct GL50   12 A6
Spa Mews GL1   4 B4
Spa Rd GL1   24 C3
Spark Hill GL11   54 B2
Sparrow Cl GL6   46 C3
Spartan Cl GL4   26 B5
Speedwell Cl GL4   26 A6
Spencer Cl GL3   26 C4
Spenser Av GL51   15 F2
Spenser Rd GL51   15 F2
Sperringate GL7   61 E5
Sperry Wy GL10   38 A5
Spey Cl GL2   28 C3
Spider La GL5   41 E6
Spillmans Ct GL5   40 B6
Spillmans Pitch GL5   40 B6
Spillmans Rd GL5   40 B6
Spine Road (East) GL7   67 C6
Spine Road (West) GL7   67 A5
Spinnaker Rd GL2   24 B3
Spinney Ct GL5   45 F6
Spinney Rd GL4   26 A4
Spinning Wheel Ct GL5   39 H5
Spire Wy GL4   26 A4
Spitalgate La GL7   60 D2
Spittle Leys GL54   7 B5
Spouthouse La GL11   54 C3
Spratsgate La GL7   64 A6
Spread Eagle Ct GL1   4 E2
Spread Eagle Rd GL1   4 D2
Spring Field Ter*,
   Middle Spillmans GL5   40 B6
Spring Hill,
   Stonehouse GL10   37 B5
Spring Hill, Stroud GL6   48 B4
Spring La,
   Brimscombe GL5   45 F3
Spring La,
   Cleeve Hill GL52   9 H4
Spring La,
   Prestbury GL52   13 F1
Spring La,
   Stonehouse GL10   37 C4
Spring La, Stroud GL5   6 D4
Spring Mill Ind Est GL6   48 D5
Springbank Dr GL51   10 D6
Springbank Gro GL51   10 D6
Springbank Rd GL51   10 D6
Springbank Wy GL51   11 E5
Springdale Cl GL2   28 A6
Springfield,
   Dursley GL11   54 B4
Springfield,
   Gloucester GL2   28 B6
Springfield Cl GL51   14 C4

Springfield Ct,
   Dursley GL11   54 B4
Springfield Ct,
   Stonehouse GL10   38 C5
Springfield Rd,
   Cashes Green GL5   39 G4
Springfield Rd,
   Cirencester GL7   60 C5
Springfield Rd,
   Stroud GL5   6 D1
Springfields GL8   57 E2
Springhill GL11   54 B4
Springhill Cl GL6   48 C4
Springhill Cres GL6   48 B4
Springwell Gdns GL3   23 E2
Squires Cl GL8   46 A3
Squirrel Cl GL2   28 B6
Staites Orch GL4   31 E2
Stamages La GL6   35 F3
Stamps Mdw GL2   21 E4
Stanbury Mews GL3   27 E5
Stancombe Gro GL51   15 G6
Stancombe La GL54   7 C5
Stancombe Vw GL54   7 B5
**Standish Hospital
GL54**   **39 E2**
Stank La GL2   33 A2
Stanley House GL10   42 D1
Stanley Mills Cotts GL10   42 D1
Stanley Park GL5   43 H2
Stanley Pl GL51   11 E6
Stanley Rd,
   Cheltenham GL52   13 F6
Stanley Rd,
   Gloucester GL1   24 D5
Stanley Ter GL1   24 D5
Stanley Vw GL5   44 A1
Stanley Walk GL4   31 F4
Stanmoor GL4   30 D2
Stansby Cres GL3   22 C3
Stanthill Dr GL11   55 E7
Stanton Rd GL5   39 H4
Stanton Wy GL51   15 F3
Stantons Dr GL51   11 H2
Stanway Rd,
   Cheltenham GL51   15 E3
Stanway Rd,
   Gloucester GL4   25 H4
Stanwick Cres GL51   12 A2
Stanwick Dr GL51   12 A2
Stanwick Gdns GL51   12 A2
Star Ct GL52   12 D4
Star Hill GL6   48 A4
Star La GL8   50 B4
Starling Cl GL10   38 D4
Starveal La GL8   57 C4
Station App GL1   4 E3
Station Cl GL3   23 F4
Station Rd,
   Cheltenham GL52   8 D2
Station Rd,
   Churchdown GL3   23 F4
Station Rd, Dursley GL11   54 D3
Station Rd,
   Gloucester GL1   4 E3
Station Rd, Kemble GL7   68 B3
Station Rd,
   Nailsworth GL6   48 C4
Station Rd,
   South Cerney GL7   66 D2
Station Rd, Stroud GL5   6 B3
Station Rd,
   Woodchester GL5   44 B5
Station St GL50   5 A3
Station Vw GL10   38 B4
Staunton Cl GL4   31 E1
Staverton Technology Pk
   GL51   19 E2
Steadings Cotts GL7   60 B5
Steeple Cl GL4   26 A4
Steepstairs La GL7   61 E4
Stella Wy GL52   8 A2
Stephenson Dr GL2   33 F1
Stepping Stone La GL6   35 F3
Steps Cl GL11   54 B2
Steps La GL8   50 A4
Sterling Ct GL51   15 H1
Stevans Cl GL2   21 F4
Stevens Wy GL6   51 B1
Stewarts Mill La GL4   31 E1
Sticky La GL2   33 B2
Stirling Wy GL4   28 D3
Stirrup Cl GL2   24 A5
Stockdale Cl GL7   28 A5
Stocken Cl GL3   26 D5
Stockton Cl GL53   17 E4
Stockwell La GL52   9 F3

Stoke Orchard Rd GL52   8 A2
Stoke Park Cl GL52   8 C2
Stoke Park Ct GL52   8 C2
Stoke Rd GL52   8 A2
Stone Cl GL4   26 B4
Stone Cres GL51   11 G6
Stonebrack Piece GL4   26 A5
Stonechat Av GL4   25 H6
Stonecote Ridge GL6   46 C2
Stonecroft Cl GL52   8 B2
Stonedale Rd GL10   38 A4
Stonehenge Rd GL4   25 F4
Stonehouse Commercial
   Centre GL10   38 A5
Stonelea GL11   54 A3
Stoneleigh Cl GL53   16 C5
Stoneville St GL51   12 A4
Stoney Bri GL4   26 A5
Stoney Fld GL2   7 C1
Stony Riding GL6   46 D4
Storrington Pl GL10   38 C5
Storrington Rd GL10   38 C5
Stow Cl GL4   26 A4
Stow Ct GL51   15 H2
Stow Rd GL7   61 H1
Stow Rd, Baunton GL7   59 H3
Stowell Mews GL4   26 A4
Strachans Cl GL5   40 A5
Stratford Cl GL2   29 E1
Stratford Rd GL5   6 A2
Stratton Brook GL7   58 C6
Stratton Heights GL7   58 D5
Stratton Mills GL7   58 D6
Stratton Pl GL7   58 D6
Stratton Rd GL1   25 E3
Streamside,
   Cheltenham GL52   8 C2
Streamside,
   Gloucester GL2   28 D3
Streamside, Stroud GL5   6 D2
Strickland Rd GL52   16 D1
Stringers Cl GL5   44 B2
Stringers Dr GL51   44 B1
Stroud Court GL6   49 F5
Stroud Enterprise Centre
   GL5   44 A2
**Stroud General Hospital
GL5**   **41 E6**
**Stroud Maternity Hospital
GL5**   **41 E6**
Stroud Rd,
   Cirencester GL7   60 A4
Stroud Rd,
   Gloucester GL1   24 C3
Stroud Rd,
   Nailsworth GL6   48 A2
Stroud Rd,
   Painswick GL6   34 D6
Stroud View Ter GL5   44 C1
Stroudwater Bsns Pk
   GL10   38 A4
Stuart Ct GL6   49 G2
Stuart Ho GL6   49 G2
Studland Dr GL52   13 G3
Sturmyes Rd GL6   47 E3
Sudbrook Wy GL4   25 G6
Sudbrooke
   Trading Est GL1   4 A4
Sudeley Dr GL7   66 D2
Sudgrove Pk GL4   31 E1
Sudmeadow Rd GL2   24 A2
Suffolk Cl GL8   57 D1
Suffolk Ho GL1   4 D3
Suffolk Par GL50   16 B1
Suffolk Pl GL50   5 A6
Suffolk Rd GL50   16 A1
Suffolk Sq GL50   16 B1
Suffolk St GL50   16 B2
Sugley La GL8   51 A1
Sulgrave Cl GL4   29 E4
Summer Cl GL5   41 F5
Summer Cres GL5   41 F5
Summer St GL5   41 E5
Summerfield Cl GL51   11 G4
Summerland Dr GL3   23 F4
Summers Rd GL54   7 B5
Summersfield Cl GL6   49 H2
Summersfield Rd GL6   49 H2
Sun St GL51   12 A3
Sunderland Ct GL3   23 E4
Sunnycroft Cl GL52   8 D3
Sunnycroft Mews GL1   29 G1
Sunnyfield La GL51   14 D6
Sunnyfield Rd GL2   28 A6
Sunset La GL52   9 F6
Surrey Av GL51   15 G1
Sussex Av GL51   15 G1

Sussex Gdns GL3   27 E4
Sutton Cl GL11   55 D7
Sutton Gdns GL5   6 D4
Swallow Cl GL10   37 A5
Swallow Cres GL3   22 A2
Swallowtail Cl GL51   15 E1
Swan Ct GL1   4 B1
Swan La GL5   6 C3
Swan Rd GL1   21 E6
Swanscombe Pl GL51   15 F6
Swanswell Dr GL51   15 F3
Sweetbriar Cl GL52   8 B2
Sweetbriar St GL1   21 E6
Swells Hill GL5   45 F5
Swift Rd GL4   25 H6
Swifts Hill Vw GL5   41 E3
Swindon Cl GL51   12 A3
Swindon La GL50   12 A1
Swindon Rd,
   Cheltenham GL51   5 A1
Swindon Rd,
   Cirencester GL7   61 F3
Swindon St GL51   5 A1
Sybil Rd GL1   25 E5
Sycamore Cl GL1   29 F1
Sycamore Cres GL52   9 E2
Sycamore Ct GL51   14 D1
Sycamore Dr GL5   41 E4
Sydenham Rd GL52   12 D6
Sydenham Rd South
   GL52   12 D6
Sydenham Ter GL1   24 D5
Sydenham Villas Rd
   GL52   12 D6
Sydney GL10   38 C3
Symn La GL12   56 C3
Synwell La GL12   56 E3
Syon Rd GL6   49 H2

Tabernacle Pitch GL12   56 D2
Tabernacle Rd GL12   56 C2
Tabernacle Walk GL5   44 B2
Tabrams Pitch GL6   48 C4
Tainmor Cl GL2   22 A4
Taits Hill Rd GL11   54 A4
Talbot Mews GL1   24 C5
Talbot Rd GL51   15 H3
Talboys Walk GL8   57 D1
Tall Elms Cl GL3   22 D4
Tallis Rd GL3   22 C1
Tamar Cl,
   Cheltenham GL52   13 E4
Tamar Rd,
   Gloucester GL3   32 C2
Tamesis Dr GL7   68 B3
Tandey Walk GL3   22 C1
Tanglewood Wy GL6   46 B2
Tanners Cl GL3   32 C1
Tanners La GL51   11 F5
Tanners Piece GL6   48 C5
Tanners Rd GL51   11 F6
Tannery Cl GL10   42 B3
Tannery Cotts GL10   42 B3
Tansy Cl GL4   26 C6
Tapscott Cl GL12   56 C3
Target Cl GL5   41 F5
Tarlton Cl GL4   31 E2
Tarrington Rd GL1   25 E4
Tatchley La GL52   13 F2
Tatchley Mews GL52   13 F2
Taurus Cl GL2   28 A4
Tayberry Gro GL51   18 E1
Taylors End GL50   15 H5
Taylors Grnd GL2   28 B4
Teal Cl GL2   28 A4
Teasel Cl GL2   21 E4
Teddington Gdns GL4   25 F6
Telford Ho GL51   11 F6
Telford Wy GL2   33 D1
Teme Rd GL52   13 E5
Temple Cl GL4   26 A3
Tennyson Av GL2   29 E1
Tennyson Rd,
   Cheltenham GL51   15 F2
Tennyson Rd,
   Dursley GL11   55 F8
Tensing Rd GL53   16 C5
Tern Cl GL4   25 H5
Terry Ruck Cl GL51   15 E1
Tetbury Hill GL8   57 F4
Tetbury Hospital GL8   57 D3
Tetbury Ind Est GL8   57 E1
Tetbury La GL8   48 C5
Tetbury Rd,
   Cirencester GL7   60 A6
Tetbury Rd,
   Gloucester GL4   29 G4

Tetbury St GL6
Tewkesbury Rd,
   Cheltenham GL51
Tewkesbury Rd,
   Gloucester GL2
Thames Rd GL52
Thames Vw SN6
Thatcham Av GL2
Thatchers End GL52
The Academy GL50
The Alders GL53
The Anchorage GL2
The Ash Path GL4
The Avenue,
   Cheltenham GL53
The Avenue,
   Churchdown GL3
The Avenue,
   Cirencester GL7
The Avenue,
   Dursley GL11
The Avenue,
   Longlevens GL2
The Avenue, Stroud G
The Bank GL52
The Barge Arm GL1
The Barge Arm East G
The Bassets GL5
The Beagles GL5
The Berrells GL8
The Birches GL6
The Boulevard GL5
The Bramery GL51
The Bridgedle GL5
The Broadway,
   Dursley GL11
The Broadway,
   Oakridge GL6
The Brush GL5
The Budding GL5
The Bulwarks GL6
The Bunch of Nuts GL
The Bungalows GL5
The Burgage GL52
The Butts GL4
The Castle GL5
The Cedars GL12
The Chase,
   Gloucester GL4
The Chase, Stroud GL
The Chestnuts,
   Gloucester GL3
The Chestnuts,
   Stroud GL5
The Chipping GL8
The Churn GL6
The Circle GL5
The Cloisters GL52
The Close, Cam GL11
The Close,
   Cheltenham GL53
The Close, Coaley GL1
The Close,
   Gloucester GL2
The Close,
   Siddington GL7
The Close,
   South Cerney GL7
The Close,
   Southam GL52
The Closeoud GL12
The Common GL7
The Conifers,
   Cheltenham GL53
The Conifers,
   Gloucester GL1
The Copse GL4
The Cornfields GL52
The Corriett GL11
The Courtyard,
   Cheltenham GL50
The Courtyard,
   Gloucester GL1
The Crapen GL1
The Crescent,
   Brockworth GL3
The Crescent,
   Dursley GL11
The Crescent,
   Gloucester GL1
The Crescent,
   Stroud GL6
The Croft, Dursley GL1
The Croft, Stroud GL6
The Damsels GL8
The Dawes GL2
The Dell GL4

Vyners Cl GL7 60 D5
Vyvian Ct GL1 4 C4

Wade Ct GL51 14 D4
Wades La GL6 34 C6
Wadley Cotts GL52 17 G1
Wagers Ct GL53 17 G3
Waldrist Cl GL51 11 F4
Walham La GL2 20 D5
Walker Ct GL10 37 B5
Walkley Hill GL5 44 B1
Wallbridge GL5 6 A4
Wallbridge Ho GL5 6 A4
Walnut Cl,
   Cheltenham GL52 12 C2
Walnut Cl,
   Gloucester GL4 30 D2
Walnut Cl,
   Winchcombe GL54 7 A6
Walter Preston Ct GL5 39 H4
Walton Cl GL4 31 E2
Ward Av GL3 22 A3
Ward Cl GL52 8 D2
Warden Hill Cl GL51 15 F5
Warden Hill Rd GL51 15 F5
Wards Rd GL51 15 E5
Warns Ct GL8 57 C3
Warren Cl,
   Cheltenham GL51 15 G5
Warren Cl,
   Gloucester GL3 22 C2
Warrens Gorse Cotts
   GL7 58 B1
Warwick Av GL4 29 E4
Warwick Cl GL5 44 B2
Warwick Cres GL52 17 F2
Warwick Pl GL50 5 C2
Wasley Rd GL51 15 E2
Water La,
   Brimscombe GL5 45 F6
Water La,
   Woodchester GL5 43 H2
Water La,
   Wotton-under-Edge
   GL12 56 D3
Water St GL11 55 E6
Waterdale Cl GL2 28 A4
Waterfield Cl GL53 16 B2
Waterloo St GL51 12 A3
Watermans Ct GL2 28 A4
Watermead GL3 32 B3
Watermeadow GL2 28 B6
Watermint Dr GL2 28 D4
Watermoor Cl GL51 11 E5
Watermoor Ct GL3 22 D4
Watermoor Rd GL7 61 E4
Watermoor Wy GL7 61 F5
Waters Reach GL2 24 A5
Watershoot Cl GL52 13 E2
Waterside Cl GL2 28 A4
Waterton Cl GL3 27 E5
Waterwells Bsns Pk GL2 33 E1
Waterwells Dr GL2 33 D1
Waterwheel Cl GL2 28 A5
Watery La,
   Frampton on Severn
   GL2 36 B5
Watery La,
   Gloucester GL4 31 E5
Watledge Bank GL6 48 C3
Watledge Rd GL5 48 B2
Watson Gro GL4 31 F1
Watts Cl GL3 26 D5
Waverley Rd GL2 25 G1
Weald Cl GL4 30 C1
Weaver Brook GL6 49 E5
Weavers Cl GL11 55 D7
Weavers Croft
   Hospital GL5 40 D6
Weavers Dr GL11 51 B5
Weavers Rd,
   Cirencester GL7 61 G3
Weavers Rd,
   Gloucester GL2 28 B4
Wedgwood Dr GL2 21 H5
Weir Bridge Cl GL4 26 B3
Welch Ho*,
   Atherton GL51 11 F5
Welch Rd GL51 11 E5
Well Cross Rd GL4 30 A1

Well End GL5 41 E3
Well Hill GL6 49 G3
Well Pl GL50 12 A6
Well Walk GL50 5 B3
Welland Ct GL52 13 E3
Welland Dr GL52 13 E3
Welland Lodge Rd GL52 13 E2
Welland Rd GL2 28 B3
Wellbrook Rd GL52 8 D1
Wellesley Rd GL50 5 C1
Wellesley St GL1 25 E5
Wellington Ho GL7 61 E3
Wellington La GL52 5 D2
Wellington Par GL1 4 E2
Wellington Rd GL52 5 D1
Wellington Sq GL50 5 C1
Wellington St,
   Cheltenham GL50 5 C5
Wellington St,
   Gloucester GL1 4 D4
Wells Cl GL51 15 G6
Wells Rd,
   Gloucester GL4 25 H3
Wells Rd, Stroud GL6 46 C1
Wellsprings Rd GL2 21 G6
Welsh Wy GL7 58 B1
Welveland La GL4 26 A2
Welwyn Mews GL51 15 E6
Wendover Gdns GL50 15 H2
Wentworth Cl,
   Cheltenham GL51 11 E6
Wentworth Cl,
   Gloucester GL2 21 G4
Wentworth Rd GL51 11 E6
Wesley Ct GL5 6 D3
Wesley Rd GL10 42 B3
Wessex Dr GL52 13 F5
West Approach Dr GL52 12 D2
West Court Grange GL5 6 B1
West Dr GL50 5 D1
West End, Dursley GL11 54 A3
West End,
   Minchinhampton GL6 49 F2
West End La GL3 27 E5
West Fld GL2 7 C1
West Hay Gro GL7 68 B3
West La GL7 68 B3
West Lodge Dr GL4 26 A5
West Market Pl GL7 61 E3
West Quay GL1 4 A3
West St GL8 57 C3
West Tynings GL6 48 B4
West Vw GL12 56 E2
West Wy GL7 61 E3
Westal Ct GL51 15 H4
Westal Pk GL51 15 H4
Westbourne Dr,
   Cheltenham GL52 12 D5
Westbourne Dr,
   Gloucester GL2 28 A6
Westbury Rd,
   Cheltenham GL51 16 C4
Westbury Rd,
   Gloucester GL2 28 A6
Westcote Rd GL4 29 G4
Westdown Gdns GL52 12 D5
Westend GL11 53 G5
Westend Par GL1 20 B6
WestendTer GL1 20 B6
Western Rd GL50 12 A5
Westfield GL11 55 C6
Westfield Av GL3 32 A1
Westfield Rd GL3 32 A2
Westfield Ter GL2 20 D4
Westfields GL12 56 C3
Westgate St GL1 4 A1
Westland Rd GL2 33 B1
Westmead Rd GL2 22 A4
Westminster Cl GL53 16 D1
Westminster Ct GL2 25 G1
Weston Rd GL1 24 D3
Westover Ct GL3 22 D2
Westridge Rd GL12 56 C2
Westrip La GL5 39 G4
Westrip Pl GL5 39 G4
Westward Ct GL5 39 G6
Westward La GL5 39 F6
Westwood La GL2 13 H3
Wetherleigh Dr GL2 7 C1
Weyhouse Cl GL5 41 E6

Whaddon Av GL52 13 E5
Whaddon Dr GL52 12 D4
Whaddon Rd GL52 12 D4
Wharf Ho GL5 6 A4
Wharfdale Sq GL51 11 G6
Wharfdale Wy GL10 38 B6
Wheat Hill GL8 57 B2
Wheatland Dr GL51 11 F4
Wheatridge Ct GL4 30 D1
Wheatsheaf Dr GL52 8 B2
Wheatstone Ct GL2 33 D1
Wheatstone Rd GL1 25 E4
Wheatway GL4 30 D2
Wheelers Rise GL5 40 A4
Wheelers Walk GL5 40 A4
Whips La GL8 48 B3
White Cross Sq GL53 16 C2
White Hall GL5 41 E5
White Wy GL7 59 E3
Whitebeam Cl GL2 21 G4
Whitecourt GL11 51 A5
Whitecroft GL6 48 B4
Whitefield Cl GL50 38 C6
Whitefields Rd GL52 8 B2
Whitefriars La GL7 67 C5
Whitehart St GL51 12 A4
Whitehorse La GL6 35 G2
Whitehouse Pk GL5 39 H6
Whitehouse Wy GL52 9 E3
Whitelands Rd GL7 61 F3
Whitemarsh Cl GL51 11 E4
Whitethorn Dr GL52 13 F4
Whiteway GL11 55 F8
Whiteway Cl GL11 55 E8
Whiteway Rd GL4 30 B1
Whiteway Vw GL7 58 D6
Whitewell Cl GL4 26 B4
Whitfield St GL1 4 E3
Whitminster La GL2 36 B3
Whitmore Rd GL54 7 A4
Whittington Rd GL51 14 D3
Whittle Av GL4 29 F4
Whittle Cl GL51 14 D2
Whittles La GL2 36 A5
Whitworth Rd GL7 61 E4
Whornes Orch GL4 31 E2
Wick St GL6 35 F5
Wickridge Cl GL5 40 D4
Wickwater La GL7 66 F4
Widden St GL1 4 F4
Wiggold Cotts GL7 59 H4
Wigmore Cl GL4 26 B5
Wildmoorway La GL7 66 E2
Wilkes Av GL3 26 C3
Wilkinson Rd GL7 61 E6
Willcox Dr GL52 9 E3
Willersey Rd GL51 15 E3
William Gough Cl GL51 11 E4
Williams Orch GL2 7 B2
Willow Av, Dursley GL11 55 D6
Willow Av,
   Gloucester GL4 25 G4
Willow Cl,
   Cheltenham GL52 9 E3
Willow Cl, Dursley GL11 54 D4
Willow Croft Cl GL4 30 C3
Willow Ct GL5 6 C2
Willow Dr GL52 9 E3
Willow Gro GL7 66 D2
Willow Park Dr GL52 8 C1
Willow Rd,
   Charlton Kings GL53 17 F4
Willow Rd,
   Cheltenham GL52 13 F6
Willow Rd,
   Kings Stanley GL10 42 D2
Willow Rd,
   Stonehouse GL10 38 B5
Willow Wy GL4 25 G5
Willowbrook Dr GL51 11 E4
Willowherb Cl GL52 13 G3
Willowleaze GL2 22 A6
Wilson Rd GL51 18 C3
Wilton Cl GL1 24 C6
Wilton Rd GL1 24 C6
Wimborne Cl GL51 15 E5
Wincel Rd GL54 7 C4
Winchcombe
   Hospital GL54 7 A6
Winchcombe Rd GL4 29 G4

Winchcombe St GL52 5 C4
Winchester Dr GL4 29 G2
Winchester Wy GL51 15 G5
Windermere GL6 46 D3
Windermere Cl GL51 15 E4
Windermere Rd,
   Cheltenham GL51 15 F4
Windermere Rd,
   Gloucester GL2 21 H5
Windfall Wy GL2 25 H1
Windmill Cotts,
   Gloucester GL1 25 F2
Windmill Cotts,
   Kemble GL7 68 B2
Windmill Fld GL4 26 A4
Windmill Rd,
   Kemble GL7 68 B2
Windmill Rd,
   Stroud GL6 49 E1
Windrush Rd,
   Cheltenham GL52 13 E4
Windrush Rd,
   Gloucester GL4 29 E4
Windsor Dr GL4 29 E4
Windsor Rd,
   Dursley GL11 55 D6
Windsor Rd, Tetbury GL8 57 C2
Windsor St GL52 12 D4
Windsoredge La GL6 48 A3
Windyridge Gdns GL50 12 A2
Windyridge Rd GL50 12 A2
Winnycroft Cotts GL4 30 D3
Winnycroft La GL4 30 B5
Winsley Rd GL4 30 C2
Winston Rd GL3 23 E4
Winstonian Rd GL52 12 D5
Winterbotham Rd GL51 11 E6
Winton Cl GL51 15 G4
Winton Rd GL51 15 G4
Wishford Cl GL2 22 A6
Wisloe Rd GL2 52 C3
Wisteria Ct GL51 18 E1
Wisteria Rd GL8 57 C2
Wisteria Wy GL3 22 C3
Wistley Rd GL53 17 F4
Witcomb Cl GL4 31 E3
Witcombe Pl GL52 5 D5
Withy Mews GL4 25 G6
Withy Wy GL51 54 C2
Withybridge Gdns GL51 10 B1
Withybridge La GL51 10 B5
Withyfield Rd GL52 9 E2
Withyholt Cl GL53 16 D3
Withyholt Pk GL53 16 D3
Withypool GL51 15 F6
Witley Lodge Cl GL51 15 E5
Witpit La GL7 62 A5
Woburn Av GL4 29 E4
Woefuldane Bottom GL6 49 H3
Wolds La GL10 42 C2
Wolseley Rd GL2 25 G1
Wolseley Ter GL50 5 B5
Wood La GL6 48 C5
Wood Mews GL2 20 A5
Wood Stanway Dr GL52 8 C2
Woodbine Cl GL4 26 A6
Woodborough Cl GL6 35 F3
Woodcock Cl,
   Gloucester GL4 25 H6
Woodcock Cl,
   Stonehouse GL10 38 D3
Woodcock La GL10 38 C4
Woodcote GL2 21 G4
Woodend Cl GL4 26 B3
Woodend La GL11 54 A1
Woodfield Rd GL11 54 A4
Woodford Cl GL4 25 G4
Woodgate Cl,
   Cheltenham GL52 17 G3
Woodgate Cl,
   Gloucester GL4 26 B4
Woodhouse Cl GL7 60 D5
Woodhouse Dr GL5 6 B6
Woodland Av GL11 55 D5
Woodland Dr GL11 55 D5
Woodland Grn GL4 31 E2
Woodland View GL10 42 D2
Woodlands Dr GL5 41 E4
Woodlands Rd,
   Cheltenham GL51 15 H6

Woodlands Rd,
   Cirencester GL7
Woodleigh Fld GL2
Woodmancote GL11
Woodmancote Vale GL
Woodmans Wy GL52
Woodmeade Cl GL52
Woodpecker Rd GL2
Woodpecker Walk GL6
Woodrow Wy GL2
Woodruff Cl GL4
Woods Orch GL4
Woods Orchard Rd GL
Woodside La GL10
WoodstockTer GL11
Woodvale GL2
Woodview Rd GL11
Woodward Cl GL8
Woolstrop Wy GL2
Worcester Par GL1
Worcester St,
   Cheltenham GL51
Worcester St,
   Gloucester GL1
Wordsworth Av GL51
Wordsworth Rd GL11
Workmans Cl,
   The Quarry GL11
Workmans Cl,
   Tilsdown GL11
Worley Ridge GL6
Wormwood Hill GL6
Wortley Rd GL4
Wotton Cres GL12
Wotton Ct GL4
Wotton Hill GL2
Wotton Rd GL12
Wragg Castle La GL6
Wren Cl GL4
WrenTer GL3
Wychbury Cl GL53
Wye Rd GL3
Wymans La GL51
Wymans Rd GL52

Yarlington Cl GL52
YarnoldTer GL51
Yarnolds GL51
Yarrow Cl GL4
Yeend Cl GL51
Yeldham Mews GL52
Yellow Hundred Cl GL
Yew Tree Cl,
   Cheltenham GL50
Yew Tree Cl,
   Dursley GL11
Yew Tree Cotts GL4
Yew Tree Wy,
   Gloucester GL3
Yew Tree Wy, Stroud G
Yokehouse La GL6
York Rd GL4
York Row GL52
York St GL52
YorkTer GL50
Youngs Orch,
   Gloucester GL4
Youngs Orch,
   Stroud GL5
Yung Mews GL52

Zinnia Cl GL3
Zoons Rd GL3